# The CATECHISM
*Highlights & Commentary*

# The
# CATECHISM
## *Highlights &*
## *Commentary*

Brennan Hill and William Madges

XXIII
TWENTY-THIRD PUBLICATIONS
Mystic, Connecticut 06355

# Dedication

To the many faith-filled teachers and catechists
who minister to God's people throughout the world
and to the future generations of the church,
especially Ami and B.J., Katie and Sarah.

Second printing 1994

Twenty-Third Publications
185 Willow Street
P.O. Box 180
Mystic, CT 06355
(203) 536-2611
800-321-0411

ISBN 0-89622-589-5
Library of Congress Catalog Card Number 93-61482
Printed in the U.S.A.

# Preface
# How to Use This Book

The *Catechism of the Catholic Church* is the most authoritative and important catechism to be published for use in the Roman Catholic Church since the Roman Catechism of the sixteenth century. It is clearly the most significant and far-reaching church document to be issued since those of the Second Vatican Council in the 1960s. The English language edition, long delayed due to controversy concerning the translation, was eagerly anticipated by pastors, teachers, and lay readers.

Catholics all around the world are anxious to give the Catechism the careful reading it deserves. One million copies of the French edition—the first edition to be issued—were sold in less than a year. Similar brisk sales were reported for the German, Italian, and Spanish translations despite the fact that the text of the Catechism is quite long and rather difficult to read and understand. The presentation of church teachings and basic beliefs is often extremely detailed and filled with references to biblical materials and ancient Christian writers. This is appropriate for a reference book, and that is the kind of book the Catechism's authors intended to write.

But what is the person to do who wants to know the basic content of the Catechism yet is unable to sit down and read the 600-page text? What is the person to do who can read the entire text, but who does not know how it relates to the church's long history of catechesis? Where can a person turn if he or she wishes to know how contemporary theological developments relate to the content of the Catechism?

*The Catechism: Highlights & Commentary* developed out of a desire to answer these questions. It is intended to be a companion book or study guide to help people appreciate and understand the *Catechism of the Catholic Church.* It is not intended to replace the Catechism.

*The Catechism: Highlights & Commentary* begins with a brief introduction that describes the development of catechesis within the church. It details the shifts in emphasis that occurred over time and highlights the influence of particular historical periods on the shape of the church's instruction. It also relates the new catechism to several of its predecessors, including the Baltimore Catechism.

After the Introduction, *The Catechism: Highlights & Commentary* follows the exact structure of the Catechism. Likewise, the Catholic beliefs and teachings presented in this book are faithful to the tone and content of the Catechism. *The Catechism: Highlights and Commentary* uses a four-step process to explain and clarify the teachings of the Catechism:

**1. Summary:** Each major division of this book begins with a concise statement (often just one paragraph) that clearly summarizes the basic teachings contained in the corresponding portion of the Catechism.

**2. Highlights:** The complete text of the *Catechism of the Catholic Church* is over 600 pages in length. It contains thousands of references and brief quotations from the Bible, papal encyclicals, conciliar documents, Church Fathers, scholars, and saints. The language of the Catechism is often rather technical and abstract. *The Catechism: Highlights & Commentary* presents in a highly condensed manner the essential teachings of the Catechism using language that is clear, concise, and easy to understand. The numbers listed in the margins of this book refer to the corresponding numbered paragraphs in the Catechism. To explore a topic further, use the numbers in the margin of this book to refer to the detailed discussion of that issue in the Catechism.

**3. Commentary:** The Catechism was written for the universal church. The sections marked "Commentary" in *The Catechism: Highlights & Commentary* attempt to place the teachings of the Catechism into dialogue with other trends in contemporary theology. They point out how the statements of the Catechism agree with or differ from earlier church teachings and previously published church documents. The commentaries also place the basic teachings of the Catechism in the broader context of the religious and theological discussion that is taking place throughout the world today.

**4. Suggested Readings:** After each major portion of this book, several books or articles are cited. Readers wishing more information about the topics considered in a particular segment can refer to the listed books. The books were chosen because they provide further information about the contemporary discussion of issues raised in the Catechism. They are generally written in a way that is accessible to most readers.

This book is the result of collaboration among its two authors and their editor from Twenty-Third Publications, Tom Artz. William Madges wrote the Preface, Introduction, and the sections dealing with Parts Three and Four of the Catechism. Brennan Hill wrote the sections dealing with Parts One and Two, and the Conclusion. He thanks Mrs. Betti Glynn for her assistance in preparing the manuscript. Each of the authors read and commented upon the other's material, but each author bears final responsibility for what is written in his portion of the book. The authors are especially grateful to their spouses and children who endured the changes in family life that resulted from the demands of working on this project so intensely in a very short period of time.

*The Catechism: Highlights and Commentary* is suitable for a wide audience. Priests, deacons, DREs, teachers, pastoral ministers, and catechists will find the summaries, highlights, commentaries, and suggested readings most helpful when they need a quick overview of the Catechism or when they want to check a specific item. Adult Catholics, RCIA candidates, and college and high school students can use this book for personal reference or for courses and discussion programs.

It is hoped that all readers will find this book helpful in understanding the *Catechism of the Catholic Church* and in exploring their faith in its contemporary context.

# CONTENTS

# PART THREE: LIFE IN CHRIST

# PART FOUR: CHRISTIAN PRAYER

# Introduction

The publication of the *Catechism of the Catholic Church* is a landmark event. Not since the sixteenth century has the church issued a catechism for universal use. Just as that catechism, often called the "Catechism of the Council of Trent" or the "Roman Catechism," had a profound impact on Catholics for over four hundred years, so too, the publication of the *Catechism of the Catholic Church* will affect Catholic beliefs and practices around the world for the rest of our lifetime and well into the twenty-first century and beyond.

This book, which summarizes, highlights, and comments on the *Catechism of the Catholic Church*, is written to help you understand the 600-plus pages of church teachings presented in the Catechism. It also puts this document into a contemporary context and suggests avenues whereby your personal faith, ministry, or activities as a religious educator can be enriched.

In order to understand the significance of this document, it is necessary to situate it historically within the life of the church, describe its general structure, and explain its intended and appropriate use.

## Catechisms and Catechesis

The word "catechism" comes from the Greek word *(katachesis)* for oral instruction. It refers to the ancient practice of instructing people in the Christian faith. In this sense, "catechism" in one form or another has always been evident in the church as it has endeavored to tell the story of salvation from God through Christ. In fact, the church has felt itself obligated by Jesus' own intention to instruct others in the good news (see Matthew 28:18–20).

1

The church has given a different shape to "catechism" or *katachesis* in different ages. In the early church, catechism refers to the *process* of Christian instruction. Emphasis is placed on the intensive oral instruction of those who are about to be initiated into the life of the church. Over time catechism has come to refer to the *content* of that instruction. Especially in the period after the Protestant Reformation of the sixteenth century, emphasis is placed on the instruction of baptized believers. Frequent use is made of written catechetical handbooks. Today, when we hear the word "catechism" we usually think of a written book that is used as an instructional *text*.

Throughout the history of the church, catechisms, in the sense of written texts, have had two fundamental purposes: 1) to provide a concise summary of the content of Christian faith, and 2) to serve as a resource for those chiefly responsible for instructing others in the faith.

Since the Second Vatican Council (1962-65), catechesis has been understood as a multi-faceted part of the church's ministry to integrate believers into the church and to foster their relationship with God and others. *Catechesi Tradendae*, the 1979 Apostolic Exhortation of Pope John Paul II, describes catechesis this way:

> All in all, it can be taken here that catechesis is an education of children, young people and adults in the faith, which includes especially the teaching of Christian doctrine imparted, generally speaking, in an organic and systematic way, with a view to initiating the hearers into the fullness of Christian life. (#18)

## Early Church

Originally, instruction in the faith was done orally before the baptism of new converts. The New Testament, particularly the writings of Paul and Luke, speaks of people hearing the Gospel message proclaimed and then being instructed in the message and way of life of Christ. The Bible never uses the abstract noun "catechesis."

The appearance of interpretations of the good news at odds

2

with the mainline interpretation offered by the major Christian communities led to the need to formulate a precise rule of faith and to label other opinions as heresy. The Apostles' Creed, for example, reflects the need to reject those who denigrate God's act of creation or deny the humanity of Jesus. It was standard operating procedure to identify and reject heresies in favor of authentic apostolic teaching. This practice underlines the fact that at a very early stage of the church's growth catechisms and their ancient antecedents had a twofold purpose. They were to serve both as an instructional aid for teaching the faith and as a confessional statement of orthodox belief.

By the end of the second century, the church had created a distinct catechumenate, a lengthy program of initiation into the beliefs and sacramental life of the church. In the third through the fifth centuries, bishops were faced with developing a means to hand on the faith to new members of the church. When Christianity became a legally accepted religion in the Roman Empire in the early fourth century, the doors of the catechumenate were opened to larger numbers of people and the need to find effective means of passing on the faith became even more vital.

St. Augustine (ca. 354-430) was particularly influential in the development of the church's catechetical tradition. He suggested that instructional material be adapted to diverse categories of learners, and he offered some guidelines on how to approach and motivate a prospective catechumen. Augustine described the Christian life in terms of the virtues of faith, hope, and charity as exemplified in the Creed, the Lord's Prayer, and the Ten Commandments. In particular, the Apostles' Creed and Lord's Prayer were to be given to those who wanted a brief statement of what Christians believe and how they pray.

Augustine's treatment of the faith (basic beliefs) is far more extensive than his treatment of hope and love. This characteristic remains a hallmark of many later catechetical handbooks. In his treatment of love, it is interesting to note that Augustine subordinates the Ten Commandments to the gospel and emphasizes the fact that love, shed abroad in our hearts by the Holy Spirit (see Romans 5:5), is greater than faith and hope. Consequently, instead of listing the Ten Commandments, Augustine notes that the decalogue has been condensed into two commandments: to love God with our whole heart, mind, and soul and to love our neighbor as ourself. In this regard, many later catechetical works diverge from Augustine by preferring to subordinate the gospel of love to an exposition of the Ten Commandments.

## The Medieval Church

By the ninth century, the nature of catechesis had changed. Instead of having a long period of instruction for adults prior to baptism and then another period of detailed instruction afterward, the focus of catechesis shifted to children. Emphasis was placed on memorization of basic articles of the Christian faith. This change in catechesis reflected the change in the celebration of the sacrament of baptism. Infant baptism became normative throughout Europe. When baptized children were old enough to benefit from rudimentary instruction, the creed became the focal point of their Christian instruction.

From the Carolingian to the high medieval period (ninth-thirteenth centuries), numerous handbooks for Christian formation were produced for those who could read Latin. With the rise of universities and the incorporation of some aspects of Aristotelian and rational analysis in the explanation of the faith, the traditional structure of catechetical instruction was given a new justification.

Thomas Aquinas (ca. 1225-1274) explained that human salvation consists in three things: knowledge of the truth, the willing of our proper end, and the observance of virtue as the means for attaining our end. These three objectives correspond to faith, hope, and charity. Aquinas also blended church tradition and reason in his exposition of the connection between love and law.

In general, the late medieval handbooks that were designed to aid the clergy in the instruction of baptized Christians were more analytical than biblical. They explained theological terms and related Christian doctrines to one another. They focused more on the moral obligations incumbent upon believers than upon the graced quality of Christian life. They were more interested in instruction than in formation, and more effective in helping believers know the creed, decalogue, and Lord's Prayer than in living a life of faith, hope, and love.

Toward the end of the high Middle Ages, we observe the emergence of the catechism as a new and specific literary form. Whereas the term previously had referred to the *process* of Christian instruction, the term "catechism," beginning in the fourteenth century, comes to mean a book or text for such instruction. The earliest instances of this new use of the term seem to have been *The Lay Folks Catechism* of 1357, issued by the archbishop of York, and the *Catechismus Vaurensis*, a manual of instruction which the Synod of Lavaur in 1368 mandated priests to use when instructing people in the faith.

The catechisms of the fifteenth century included catalogs of sins and, in light of the horrors brought about by the Black Death, emphasized the need to prepare for death. Diedrich von Münster's *Mirror for Christians* (1470), the most widely-used Catholic catechism before and during the early years of the Reformation, emphasized the importance of the moral life and a good confession. This heavy emphasis on moral instruction was well illustrated by another contemporary work, Johannes Herolt's *Liber discipuli de eruditione Christi fidelium* (Strasbourg, 1490). This instructional guide devoted six pages to the creed, three to the Lord's Prayer, and 101 to morality under the headings of commandments, deadly sins, and various moral precepts. In the face of this moralistic environment many people felt the need for a more biblical, more experiential, and simpler instruction in the life of faith.

## The Age of Reformation

The three major Protestant Reformers—Martin Luther (1483-1546), Ulrich Zwingli (1484-1531), and John Calvin (1509-1564)—all claimed to use scripture and scripture alone as the source of authentic knowledge about what a Christian ought to do and believe. This did not mean, however, that they rejected the traditional tools the church had used to instruct believers about the basics of Christian faith. On the one hand, Luther was determined to place the Bible in the hands of every Christian who could read. Early in his career as a reformer he translated the

Bible into readable German. On the other hand, Luther realized that the Bible, even in the vernacular, did not provide a concise summary of the faith. Consequently, like many before him, he appealed to the Ten Commandments, the creed, and the Lord's Prayer as sources that taught concisely and plainly everything that was found in the scriptures.

Instead of beginning with the creed, Luther began with the commandments. This change in order reflected the existential orientation of Luther's theology. Luther's own experience as a monk had taught him that the Christian life begins with the awareness of one's own sinfulness and inability to fulfill the divine commands. As Luther saw it, the decalogue reveals our sinfulness; the creed reveals the remedy for this sinfulness, namely, divine grace and the righteousness of Christ; and the Lord's Prayer teaches us how to ask for this grace and appropriate it in our lives. This reversal of the traditional order of catechetical topics, first proposed by Luther in 1520, was embodied nine years later in his famous *Small Catechism*. This work quickly became the most influential, brief statement of the Protestant faith.

Calvin returned to the traditional order (creed, decalogue, Lord's Prayer) in his own *Catechisms* of 1537 and 1542. He made a decisive mark on the catechetical tradition, however, by emphasizing the formulation of the learner's responses. Whereas earlier catechisms were designed primarily for the teacher, Calvin's was designed for the learner. In addition, Calvin returned to the ancient practice of the church which required knowledge of the faith and its profession before active entry into the life of the church community.

The Council of Trent, which had convened in 1545 to lay out a program of reform and to respond to the theological critique of the Protestants, commissioned the writing of a new Catholic catechism. In 1566, three years after the council ended, the new catechism, originally composed in Italian, was translated into Latin. Although it is popularly known as the "Roman Catechism" or the "Catechism of the Council of Trent," its official title is the *Catechism for Parish Priests, as decreed by the Council of Trent and published by order of the Supreme Pontiff Pius V.*

As its title indicates, the Tridentine Catechism was intended to be a source book to help clergy in instructing the people. It was not a manual to be read by the faithful. As the Introduction makes clear, it presents an understanding of the Christian faith that corrected "errors" in the Protestant understanding of the faith. It was a rock-solid, "orthodox" alternative to the Protestant pamphlets and catechisms that were reaching a wide audience. This alternative to the Protestant views was not filled with subtle theological discussions, but, like the Protestant works themselves, it was biblical, comprehensible, and straightforward.

The content of the Catechism of the Council of Trent reflects the context in which it originated. The Protestant Reformers had declared that only two sacraments were authentic: baptism and the Lord's Supper. In response, the largest section of the Roman Catechism (almost 40% of the entire text) deals with the sacraments. The other three parts, on creed, decalogue, and prayer, each get about 20% of the document.

The Protestant Reformers had also accused the Church of Rome of deviating from the doctrine and discipline outlined in the Bible. To counter this attack, the Roman Catechism cites or alludes to scripture more frequently than to any other source. At the same time, it did not deny the validity of tradition in Catholic teaching. After scripture, the Catechism uses the testimony of the Fathers of the Church to define Catholic teaching St. Augustine is the author most often cited. No author who lived after St. Bernard (1090-1153) is even mentioned, except in a few very generic references.

While the first known English translation did not appear until 1829, the Catechism of the Council of Trent became the most highly authoritative, official manual of Catholic doctrine from the sixteenth to the twentieth centuries. Its authority rested upon the fact that it was decreed by an ecumenical council and approved by the pope.

## The Church in the Modern Period

The catechisms that were created in the seventeenth through the nineteenth centuries, like their predecessors, attempted to respond to the contemporary needs of the church for instruction. In the seventeenth century, catechisms continued to defend

Catholic teachings against the attacks leveled by the Protestant churches. In the eighteenth century, catechisms had to face the critical questions raised by the philosophers of the Enlightenment. In response, some catechetical works acquired a rationalistic tone as they defended the mysteries of the faith. In these catechisms there was a concomitant loss in biblical language and symbolic imagery. In the nineteenth century, a number of catechisms, appropriating the Romantic period's emphasis upon feeling and individual experience, departed from the content and format of earlier catechisms and began to focus on the individual's natural concern for self with questions like "Why did God make you?" Throughout the period, the specific tone and content of catechisms were determined by the pastoral needs of particular audiences and age groups as well as by the priorities of the bishops or religious communities which commissioned them.

Without a universal catechism, Catholic countries were left on their own to produce catechetical works appropriate to their national situation. Due to its diverse immigrant population, many different catechisms were used in the United States during the nineteenth century. Toward the end of the century, the Third Plenary Council of Baltimore (1884) mandated that a commission be appointed to prepare a general catechism whose use would be obligatory throughout the United States.

Under the direction of the committee, Monsignor Januarius de Concilio, a pastor from Jersey City who had taught theology and philosophy at Seton Hall College, completed the catechism in 1885. Although its official title is *A Catechism of Christian Doctrine, Prepared and Enjoined by Order of the Third Plenary Council of Baltimore*, the work came to be known as the "Baltimore Catechism." The catechism followed a question-and-answer format. There were 421 questions in the original version, but—due to the brevity of the answers—the text took up only 65 pages. Although the publication of the Baltimore Catechism did not completely halt the production of other Catholic catechisms, the Baltimore Catechism, in its original or revised form, did become the standard Catholic catechism for the United States and remained so until the 1960s.

A major revision of the Baltimore Catechism was begun in

1935. In 1941, after having gone through four drafts, the revised catechism was published. It now contained about 500 questions and answers (covering about 100 pages), plus an appendix of sixteen questions that constituted a brief apologetics treatise entitled "Why I am a Catholic." The revision and expansion of the text did not incorporate the new approaches to biblical studies being attempted in the mid-twentieth century, but did reflect the growing catechetical movement and the desire for convert-making. The Baltimore Catechism was the principal tool of religious instruction for countless Catholic children and adult converts until the Second Vatican Council in the mid-1960s.

In the preparatory stages of Vatican II, the question of a common catechism for the worldwide church was raised again. Such a catechism was not discussed at the Council itself. Instead, the Council mandated a "directory" that would offer general norms and principles for catechesis. Before the new catechetical directory appeared, the Dutch bishops issued their *New Catechism* (1965). It received critical acclaim and wide distribution both in Holland and the English-speaking world because it expressed the new theological insights of Vatican II in a way that was not only intelligible, but also appealing to many adults.

Acting on the mandate of the Second Vatican Council, Pope Paul VI approved the *General Catechetical Directory* in March, 1971. The Directory summarized the organizing principles and guidelines to be used for catechesis throughout the universal church. Two principles have special relevance as church leaders and educators implement the teachings of the *Catechism of the Catholic Church*. First, the instruction of adults is to be the model for all forms of catechesis. Second, the content and method of instruction should be formulated so that it is appropriate for the particular people and culture for whom it is intended.

To facilitate the development of appropriate catechetical formation throughout the world, national episcopal conferences were encouraged to prepare directories that applied these general principles and guidelines to the specific needs of their own country. *Sharing the Light of Faith: The National Catechetical Directory for Catholics of the United States* (1979) is the U.S. Catholic bishops' response to this directive. Among hopeful signs in contemporary catechesis within the United States, the Directory identifies contemporary developments in the sacred and human sciences, attention to social justice, renewed interest in the Bible and liturgy, and the assumption by lay people of increased responsibility and leadership in catechetical work.

## The New Catechism

The publication of the *Catechism of the Catholic Church* is a decisive development in the church. It is designed to become an important new resource in the catechetical ministry of the church. Unlike the *General Catechetical Directory*, it does not deal with catechetical methodology (principles and guidelines for catechesis), but deals rather with catechetical content (Christian truths to be taught). The *Catechism of the Catholic Church* is the first major catechism to be issued with papal support for use by the entire church since the Catechism of the Council of Trent was promulgated in the mid-sixteenth century. Undoubtedly, this catechism will be used to shape the faith of those who will live in the twenty-first century.

The proximate source of the Catechism's creation was the extraordinary Synod of Bishops convened in 1985 by the pope. Cardinal Bernard Law of Boston introduced the idea of a catechism on the very first day of the Synod. The Final Report of the Synod records the desire of the synod participants "that a catechism or compendium of all catholic doctrine regarding both faith and morals be composed as a source text for the catechisms or compendia composed in the various countries." The presentation of the faith was to be biblical and liturgical, "presenting sure teaching adapted to the actual life of Christians." (*Final Report*, II. B. A. 4.)

As is well known, Vatican II embarked on some new ground—in its understanding of the nature of the church and the role of the laity, in its understanding of the relationship between the Catholic church and other Christian communions and other religions, in its understanding of religious freedom. Whereas some might emphasize the fact that these positions underscore Vatican II's intent to express the faith more appropriately in its modern context, Pope John Paul II feels that Vatican II also had as part of its "main task" the mission of guarding the deposit of Christian teaching more effectively.

The Apostolic Constitution *Fidei Depositum* announcing the publication of the *Catechism of the Catholic Church* sheds light on the pope's intentions and hopes for the catechism. First, Pope John Paul II hopes that the Catechism will help to revive and renew the faith of God's people. In order to do this, it will have to include in its presentation of the faith both the new and the old. Second, the pope wants the Catechism to serve the church by providing a statement of faith that will "strengthen the bonds of unity" in the church. The Catechism is expected to achieve this task insofar as it is used as "a sure and authentic source book for the teaching of Catholic doctrine and especially for the composition of local catechisms." (*Fidei Depositum*, #4) The pope makes it clear that this catechism is not intended to replace local catechisms approved by ecclesiastical authorities, but is intended to encourage the writing of new local catechisms "which take into account the different situations and cultures but which carefully guard the unity of the faith and fidelity to Catholic doctrine." (*Fidei Depositum*, #4)

The *Catechism of the Catholic Church* is the result of six years of work. In 1986 the pope established a commission of twelve cardinals and bishops, over which Cardinal Ratzinger presided, to prepare a plan for the catechism. An editorial committee of seven additional bishops assisted this commission in its work. All the Catholic bishops of the world, as well as a number of theologians, catechetical and theological institutions, were consulted during the preparation of this text. The text went through nine drafts before its final form was approved by Pope John Paul II in June, 1992, and officially promulgated in December of that year. The first edition of the Catechism was issued in French. More than a year elapsed before the English edition was released in 1994.

## Using the Catechism

The *Catechism of the Catholic Church* is intended to be used as one means of instruction in the Christian faith. Although a privileged means, it is not the exclusive means. As the Prologue makes clear, the Catechism is intended primarily for bishops in their role as teachers and pastors. Through the bishops, the Catechism is also addressed to all others responsible for instruction in the faith. The Catechism presents an official summary of those teachings which the ministry of catechesis seeks to impart.

The new catechism arranges its content in thematic order, and thus follows a very popular arrangement in the history of catechesis. The catechism begins with what the church believes, then moves to consider what the church celebrates, lives, and prays. Part One, the Profession of Faith, presents the main tenets of the creed. Part Two, the Celebration of the Christian Mystery, presents the sacramental life of the church. Part Three, Life in Christ, deals with the moral teaching of the church. Part Four, Christian Prayer, offers a brief history of prayer and presents the church's teaching on the kinds of prayer and its role in the Christian life.

It is interesting to note the space allotted to the four central topics in different catechisms. In the Roman Catechism of the sixteenth century the discussion of the sacraments received twice as much space (40%) as any other topic because it was the issue being contested most strongly by the reformers. The three remaining topics (creed, commandments, Lord's Prayer) each received about the same amount of space (20% each). Today's *Catechism of the Catholic Church* devotes about 39% of the text to a discussion of the creed. It then allots unequal amounts of space to the other major topics: 27% to morality, 23% to the sacraments, and only 11% to prayer. This reflects the concern of Catholic church officials in Rome with regard to certain contemporary trends in theological teaching and ethics.

Although the Catechism attempts to present its content without reference to any particular culture, it is important to recognize that every expression—even when explicitly intending a universal expression—bears the marks of the culture in which it was created and the language it uses. The Catechism itself acknowledges that adaptation of the text to the differences of culture, age, social and ecclesial condition is indispensable. The challenge of a CCD teacher or RCIA catechist remains the same after the publication of the Catechism as before: to present the basic teachings of the faith and Christian life in a manner that is understandable and in keeping with the level of intelligence and experience of the student or inquirer.

It is worthwhile to recall the advice of the seventeenth-century church historian Claude Fleury (1640-1723) concerning the best use of a catechism. He suggests that the fundamental purpose of a catechism is to enable Christians to take an *active* part in the life of the Christian community and to *benefit* from it. Minimally, that means helping people to understand the basics of the story of salvation and to participate sacramentally in the celebration of this story. From this perspective, a good catechism can enrich the faith lives of Christians; it is not an end in itself. As others have pointed out, knowledge of sound doctrine, although important, is not the same thing as mature faith. The new catechism will be salutary in the life of the church if it is used to promote and enrich mature faith among God's people.

## Suggested Readings

Augustine, Saint. *The Enchiridion on Faith, Hope, and Love*. South Bend, IN: Gateway Editions, 1961.

Bradley, Robert I. *The Roman Catechism in the Catechetical Tradition of the Church: The Structure of the Roman Catechism as Illustrative of the "Classical Catechesis."* Lanham, MD: University Press of America, 1990.

*Communio: International Catholic Review* (1983) 10. Essays on catechesis, catechisms, and faith by Karl Lehmann, Hans Urs von Balthasar, Joseph Cardinal Ratzinger, and Guy Bedouelle.

Janz, Denis. *Three Reformation Catechisms: Catholic, Anabaptist, Lutheran.* New York: Edwin Mellen Press, 1982.

John Paul II, Pope. *Fidei Depositum*. Washington, DC: United States Catholic Conference, 1993.

Marthaler, Berard. "The Catechism Genre, Past and Present," in *World Catechism or Inculturation?* Johann-Baptist Metz and Edward Schillebeeckx, eds. Edinburgh: T & T Clark, 1989.

National Conference of Catechetical Leadership. *Implementing the Catechism of the Catholic Church: A Resource for Diocesan and Parish Catechetical Leaders and Publishers of Catechetical Materials.* Washington, DC: NCCL, 1993.

Paul VI, Pope. *General Catechetical Directory*. Washington, DC: United States Catholic Conference, 1971.

Reese, Thomas J., ed. *The Universal Catechism Reader: Reflections and Responses*. San Francisco: HarperSanFrancisco, 1990.

United States Catholic Conference. *Sharing the Light of Faith: The National Catechetical Directory for Catholics in the United States*. Washington, DC: United States Catholic Conference, 1979.

Warren, Michael, ed. *Sourcebook for Modern Catechetics*. Winona, MN: St. Mary's Press, 1983.

# PART ONE

# THE
# PROFESSION
# OF
# FAITH

# Section One:
# I Believe - We Believe

**Summary**

This section defines what it means to believe or to have faith. It explains that faith is a human response, a personal and free commitment to the self-revelation of God. God's gratuitous and free self-revelation invites all people to the knowledge of God and the acceptance of salvation. The pinnacle of God's self-revelation is found in the person of Christ whose message lives on in Scripture and Tradition. An individual's response of faith is rooted in the God-given capacity to seek God in the world, especially through human persons who are made in God's image and likeness. One of the chief functions of the Catholic community is to nurture the faith of its members.

# Chapter One:
# The Human Capacity for God
### (n. 26-49)

26-29    God has placed in the human heart a desire to be united to the Creator, and God continually draws individuals on. This religious search is common to all people, and yet individuals are free to reject an intimate relationship with God.

While there are no scientific proofs for God's existence,    31-33
there are many aspects of the world's order and beauty
which render God's existence probable.

Human faculties help people know of the existence of    35-38
a personal God, but it is revelation and grace which
bring them into a true intimacy with God.

Human knowledge and language are limited. People    40-42
speak about God in relation to creatures since all creatures bear some resemblance to God. Yet God is
Mystery, and thus beyond all language and imagery.

# Chapter Two:
# God's Initiative - Revelation
### (n. 50-184)

Through revelation God makes it possible for in-    52
dividuals to respond to God and to know and love
God in a way that is far beyond the response that is
possible solely from natural reason.

God's self-communication is addressed to all hu-    53-56,
mankind and culminates in the person and mission of    66, 74
Jesus Christ. God's covenant reaches all people and the
divine plan of salvation is intended for all nations.
Even though revelation is complete, Christians continue to explore it and to grasp its significance more
fully over time.

God's self-communication through Jesus, the eternal    79, 82
Word, is present and active in the church. Scripture
and Tradition are distinct, yet closely related. Both

flow from God's self-communication and together they make present the mystery of Jesus Christ.

85-90     The teaching authority of the church protects and interprets God's Word. This teaching authority, however, is the servant of the Word and not superior to it. Within Catholic teaching there is an order or "hierarchy of truths" in which defined dogmas are the fullest expression of the church's teaching authority.

92-93     Guided by the teaching authority of the church, the community possesses a certain sense of the faith. The community of the faithful as a body of believers filled with the Spirit cannot err in matters of belief.

103-10,   The church honors the Scriptures as it honors the Body
119       of Christ. The books of scripture were written under the inspiration of the Holy Spirit. In order to find the intention of the authors, one must take into account the times, cultures, and literary genres that were current when the individual books of the Bible were written. The function of scripture scholars is to help the church's understanding of scripture grow and deepen.

153, 166  Faith is a divine gift, a grace from God that enables us to make an authentic human act of faith. It is a personal act, yet an act linked to the faith of others.

158-164   Faith seeks to know God better and to understand and love God. It is a free response, made not by coercion but in conscience. Faith needs to be nourished, especially today when there is so much that challenges faith.

## Commentary

In describing the human person and the human person's relationship to God, the Catechism moves away from the older dualistic description of human nature wherein the supernatural built upon the natural. The Catechism adopts an anthropology in which the chasm between the human and divine is bridged by the creative act of God. It is this action which gives the human heart its desire to be with God. Religion, then, is not extrinsic to human beings, but is universally integral to human nature.

Echoed here is the teaching of the First Vatican Council (1869-70) that the existence of God can be known by reason, but that revelation and grace are needed both for a fuller understanding of God and for intimacy with God. Karl Rahner, the twentieth-century Jesuit theologian, moved beyond this view by proposing that people have been created in "openness to God." He explained that human nature bears a "supernatural existential" which enables people to find God as the answer to their questions and the ground of human experience. Bernard Lonergan, another twentieth-century Jesuit theologian, proposed that there is indeed a level of human consciousness whereby people can reach out to God. Other theologians have offered similar methods for more closely co-relating humans and their culture with God as their accepted horizon. They point out that all creation, and uniquely human beings, has been "graced" with God's presence and power.

The Catechism reflects the fact that Catholics have generally moved away from attempts to prove God's existence, and yet it still maintains that faith is reasonable. Events of nature, "reasons of the heart," and human experience can all point to the existence of God. For its part, liberation theology proposes that one can discover God's self-communication as the liberator in the experience of poverty and oppression.

The Mystery of God is beyond concepts, language, and story. People question and search for meaning using analogy, metaphor, and statements of belief. While the tradition authoritatively transmits the substance of revelation, the forms change, the interpretations vary, and the doctrine develops throughout the history of the church.

Revelation, or the self-communication of God, is understood to be given to all. This perspective, reflective of the tone of the Second Vatican Council (1962-1965), promotes a deeper respect for the truth claims of other churches and religions. It also alerts people to be attentive to revelation as it emerges through personal and communal experience and through human culture. Christian revelation, while complete, needs to be explored constantly in order to grasp more fully its significance. The importance of the ministry of catechesis for helping the faithful in this exploration becomes quite evident.

The Catechism reflects the distinction made at the Second Vatican Council that Scripture and Tradition are not viewed as "two sources" of revelation, but as two distinct, yet related ways in which God is revealed. The church, which existed before the scriptures were written and which had to determine which texts authentically conveyed the apostolic tradition, is nonetheless "servant" to the Word of God. The church's dogmatic tradition must be faithful to biblical revelation. Over fifty years of contemporary biblical scholarship have provided insights that opened the way to newer and deeper understandings of the Catholic tradition. One wishes that contemporary exegesis would have been used much more extensively in the Catechism. Scripture in the Catechism tends to be used in the more traditional form of "proof texts."

The Catechism makes a useful distinction between the gift of faith and the personal and free act of faith. Contemporary theology looks beyond this to the many dimensions of a holistic response of faith. Such a response is made not only rationally, but with the emotions, imagination, will, and aesthetic sense. Active faith, especially faith actively expressed in the cause for social justice, has been in the forefront in both theology and religious education's understanding of the appropriate lived expression of one's faith.

Faith needs to be perceived as personal and relational. Both theologians and religious educators have used psychology, sociology, anthropology, and other secular sciences to better understand the phenomenon of faith. They explain that faith develops through various stages, and that gender is an important factor in faith development. These perspectives have been most helpful to religious educators in their ministry to the faithful of the community and can serve to expand the narrower perspective offered in the Catechism.

## Suggested Readings

**Revelation**

Dulles, Avery. *Models of Revelation.* Garden City, NY: Doubleday, 1985.

Haught, John. *Mystery and Promise: A Theology of Revelation.* Collegeville, MN: Liturgical Press, 1993.

Perkins, Pheme. *Reading the New Testament.* Revised edition. Mahwah, NJ: Paulist Press, 1988.

**Faith**

Chamberlain, Gary. *Fostering Faith: A Minister's Guide to Faith.* Mahwah, NJ: Paulist Press, 1988.

Hill, Brennan, Paul Knitter, and William Madges. *Faith, Religion, and Theology.* Mystic, CT: Twenty-Third Publications, 1990.

Kasper, Walter. *Introduction to Christian Faith.* Mahwah, NJ: Paulist Press, 1980.

**General Works**

Cunningham, Lawrence. *The Catholic Faith: An Introduction.* Mahwah, NJ: Paulist Press, 1987.

Rahner, Karl. *Foundations of Christian Faith.* New York: Crossroad, 1982.

Marthaler, Berard. *The Creed.* Revised edition. Mystic, CT: Twenty-Third Publications, 1993.

# Section Two: The Creed

## Chapter One: I Believe in God the Father
### (n. 185-421)

### Summary

This chapter deals with the one living God who is merciful and gracious. God is described as a God of truth and love who has been revealed as Father, Son, and Spirit. God has created and ordered a good world founded on wisdom and love. God sustains creation according to a mysterious and providential plan, and calls creatures to cooperate in this plan. Although God is almighty and powerful, God permits evil but can bring good out of evil. The experience of evil and suffering can give the appearance that God is absent and even powerless. This is not the case. Only faith can deal with these mysteries. The chapter goes on to explain that all creatures reflect the goodness of God. Humans are the summit of creation and are called to be stewards of creation. In this context, original sin is described as the abuse of freedom and the rejection of God's goodness that then implicates and affects all people.

### I Believe in God the Father Almighty (n. 199-278)

200-202   God is revealed as one and unique. This was confirmed by Jesus who taught that people should love God with all their heart, soul, mind, and strength.

203-207   God is not an anonymous force, but a living God, who revealed the divine essence and identity in the name Yahweh (I am). God is hidden in mystery, beyond time and space. God is the fullness of being and perfection, the Holy One who is a constant saving presence for the people.

215-217   God is a God of truth and fidelity, One who is always faithful to divine promises. God's wisdom governs the world. God's truth is contained in revelation, especially in the revelation of the Son, Jesus Christ.

218-221   God's love for all people is eternal; stronger than either a father's love, mother's love, or the love of a spouse. God's very being is love, and this love is affirmed in the sending of the Son, Jesus Christ. God's parental tenderness can be described in images of both a father's love and a mother's love.

223-225   To believe in God is to live in service, thanksgiving, and trust. People who believe in God are aware that all things find the source of their existence in God. True belief realizes the unity and dignity of all people.

The central mystery of Christian faith and life is the    237-244
Trinity, which is the revelation of God as Father, Son,
and Spirit. Jesus is the visible image of the invisible
God; the Spirit is sent by the Father in the name of the
Son.

One of God's attributes is almighty power, a power    268-270
that is creative, loving, caring, and forgiving.

God can seem absent in times of evil, but faith enables    272-273
people to grasp the mysteriousness of God's power.
Christ's resurrection after his death on the cross reveals God's power over evil.

### The Creator (n. 279-324)

Creation is the foundation of God's plan of salvation.        280
Christ is the culmination of this plan, as well as the one
who reveals its final goal in a new creation.

Scientific studies of human origins enrich people's    283-284
knowledge and can also increase their admiration for
the Creator. Faith tells them that a good God created
the universe and that it did not come about through
chance or fate.

Creation and covenant are integrally related. Creation        288
is a first step toward covenant; it is the initial and universal witness to the all-powerful love of God.

The biblical accounts of creation as found in the Book        289
of Genesis originate in diverse literary sources yet they
succeed in expressing the truths of creation: its origin
and end in God, its order and goodness, the vocation

of humankind, the drama of sin, and the hope of salvation.

290-294    God alone is the Creator. Creation is the work of the Trinity: God creates through and for the Son; the Spirit of God is the creative source of life and good. Creation communicates the glory and goodness of God.

295-300    Creation is not the product of blind fate or chance, nor did anything exist before creation. God freely and wisely created an orderly and good world. God transcends creation, and yet is present to it.

301-302,   God sustains the process of creation with a caring and
307        protecting providence. God empowers people to share freely and responsibly in the plan of providence.

310-312    God did not create a perfect world, but a world in the state of becoming with both physical goods and evils. God does not cause moral evil, but permits it in light of human freedom, and can derive good from the consequences of evil.

*Heaven and earth (n. 325-421)*

332-334    Angels have been present from the dawn of creation and throughout the history of salvation. The mysterious and powerful help of angels is a benefit to the life of the church.

337-339    The world in all its richness and diversity was created by God. Every creature has a unique goodness and perfection, and in its own way is a reflection of God. The goodness of every creature must be respected.

340-341    All creatures, including the sun and the moon, the flower and the sparrow are interdependent. There is a hierarchy of creatures, yet God loves them all and takes care of each one. The beauty of the universe reflects the beauty of God.

Human beings are the summit of God's creation. 343, Created in the image of God and possessing the dignity of personhood, human beings are intended to live in solidarity with all creatures since everything comes from the same Creator. In a special way, they stand in solidarity as brothers and sisters to one another.

343,
357-361

The human person has been created by God as body and spirit, as one and whole. Both body and spirit share in being the image of God.

362-364

God created and willed woman and man in perfect equality. Both are created in the image of God with equal dignity. They are complementary to one another. In marriage they are one, and uniquely cooperate in God's creative work of communicating human life.

369-372

Both woman and man are stewards of the earth. Their dominion over creation, however, is not to be arbitrary and destructive, but should be loving and responsible.

373

The first parents were created as good, in harmony with God and all of creation, in a state of original holiness and justice. Sin is an abuse of the freedom that people have to love God and one another. The first parents fell from grace through disobedience and an abuse of freedom.

374, 387,
397

All humans are somehow implicated in original sin. As a result of this, human nature is wounded. It is subject to ignorance, suffering, and death. It manifests an inclination toward evil. Jesus Christ has conquered sin and evil, and has set us free from the power of original sin.

402-407

## Commentary

The Catechism points out that God is not an anonymous force for Catholics, but a living, loving, and saving presence. It acknowledges at the same time that this God is Mystery, and beyond our temporal and spatial considerations. It deems both feminine and masculine images as acceptable ways to describe God's love. Inter-faith dialogue, liberation theology, process thought, and feminist theology have suggested many alternative possibilities for imaging God beyond those mentioned in the Catechism. Whereas in the past there was a stress on the transcendence of God, the emphasis today seems to have shifted to the immanence of God. This shift is most evident in the current effort to link Christian theology with ecological concerns—a concern duly noted in the pages of the Catechism.

Traditional notions of providence have been severely challenged by horrors such as the Holocaust and countless other acts of violence and injustice. The world is often plagued by massive natural disasters and destruction. The phenomenon of human freedom brings evils, both physical and moral. God's power in and over the world does, as the Catechism indicates, have to be viewed as loving, caring, and forgiving, and not as the power responsible for evil.

For a broader perspective we can turn to liberation theology which has resisted accepting oppression as "God's will" or as something permitted by God. God is viewed as a liberator empowering the oppressed to confront evil and shape their own destiny by bringing to fruition God's kingdom. Process thought offers another perspective on God's role amid suffering by suggesting that God is a "fellow-sufferer" who stands in solidarity with humankind in the midst of their suffering and oppression.

The Catechism gives prominence to the Trinity. This emphasis on trinitarian theology is certainly grounded in the Christian tradition, although at times the Trinity has been given less emphasis. When addressing the mystery of the Trinity today, many theologians stress the communitarian aspects of the Trinity, and search for ways to include feminine images and language in the description of the inner life of God.

Contemporary scientific findings are not the threat to Catholic thinking that they were from the time of Galileo up to the last century. Today it is understood that the Genesis stories are not factual or scientific accounts of creation, but instead profess faith in God as the creator of a world that is essentially good. Scientific findings with regard to evolution and the origin of the universe are viewed as compatible with and complementary to Christian teachings on creation. Theologians have built upon the foundational work of Teilhard de Chardin and others to relate scientific findings to the Christian tradition. Pope John Paul II has periodically addressed gatherings of scientists and has encouraged mutual respect and cooperation between religion and science.

Twentieth-century biblical exegesis has offered valuable insights on the sources and original meaning of the creation stories in the Book of Genesis. From this perspective, the ancient myths symbolized in Adam and Eve and the story of the Fall show how sin has been part of humankind from the beginning. Original sin is seen as a universal tendency to sin, a tendency that is influenced by the sinful structures into which all people are born. Some theologians hold that this view seems to be more compatible with the findings of contemporary anthropology and social sciences than the view found in the Catechism that speaks of a historical fall from a state of original justice.

The goodness of each created reality, the unique reflection of God in every single creature, and the interdependence of all are valuable truths for addressing the environmental crises that we face today. Responsible stewardship, rather than domination and exploitation, is of utmost importance for sustaining and renewing the earth at this crucial period of history. The dignity of each person, and especially of the poor who are so adversely affected by pollution and exploitation also needs to be stressed at this time. While the Catechism makes passing reference to these ecological concerns, many theologians suggest that we shift our perspective so that being more "earth-centered" than "human-centered" is central to one's worldview.

Likewise today there is a profound awakening to the truth of the equality of the genders. Both women and men have been created in the image and likeness of God and are called to live and work together in solidarity with each other. This truth is gradually dawning on people in all cultures and religions, and is noted in the text. It is a truth that calls for major reforms in all institutions, most especially in the church, which stands as a sacrament of God's creative presence and should lead the way in freedom and equality.

# Suggested Readings

**God**

Gallagher, Michael. *Losing God*. Mystic, CT: Twenty-Third Publications, 1992.

Haught, John. *What is God?* Mahwah, NJ: Paulist Press, 1986.

Hill, William J. *Search for the Absent God*. New York: Crossroad, 1992.

Johnson, Elizabeth. *She Who Is*. New York: Crossroad, 1992.

Kasper, Walter. *The God of Jesus Christ*. New York: Crossroad, 1984.

LaCugna, Catherine. *God for Us: The Trinity and Christian Life*. San Francisco: HarperSanFrancisco, 1991.

**Creation**

Hayes, Zachary. *What are They Saying About Creation?* Mahwah, NJ: Paulist Press, 1980.

Johnson, Elizabeth. *Women, Earth and Creator Spirit*. Mahwah, NJ: Paulist Press, 1993.

Moltmann, Jurgen. *God in Creation*. Minneapolis: Augsburg Fortress, 1993.

**Science and Creation**

Capra, Fritjof, and David Stendl-Rast. *Belonging to the Universe: Explorations on the Frontiers of Science and Spirituality*. San Francisco: HarperSanFrancisco, 1992.

**Ecology**

Lonergan, Anne, and Caroline Richards, eds. *Thomas Berry and the New Cosmology*. Mystic, CT: Twenty-Third Publications, 1987.

McFague, Sallie. *The Body of God*. Minneapolis: Augsburg Fortress, 1993.

Reuther, Rosemary Radford. *Gaia and God: An Ecofeminist Theology of Earth Healing*. San Francisco: HarperSanFrancisco, 1992.

# Chapter Two:
# I Believe in Jesus Christ,
# the Only Son of God
### (n. 422-682)

## Summary

This chapter begins with the announcement of the good news that God sent the Son to save us, and then summarizes the central teachings about the person and nature of Jesus. The text explains that the titles "Jesus," "Christ," "Only Son of God," and "Lord" proclaim Jesus' identity as messiah and divine savior. The Incarnation is the belief that the Son of God became a human being. Jesus Christ is both human and divine. He was conceived of the Virgin Mary by the power of the Holy Spirit. Redemption is at work in all the events or mysteries of Jesus Christ's life: his birth, life in Nazareth, baptism, temptations, preaching, miracles, death, resurrection, and ascension.

*Jesus Christ (n. 422-483)*

Jesus of Nazareth was born a Jew, worked as a carpenter, and died by crucifixion in Jerusalem. Jesus of Nazareth is the eternal Son of God made flesh, the Messiah, the Christ.    423-424

Belief in Jesus Christ stands at the heart of catechesis. The aim of catechesis is to put people in intimate touch with Jesus Christ and his teachings.    426

Jesus ("Joshua" in Hebrew; "Jesus" in Greek) means "God saves." In Jesus, God sums up the history of salvation of all people. The name "Jesus" signifies that God's own name is present in the person of the Son. This is the divine name that alone brings salvation. Jesus' resurrection glorifies the name of God the Savior.    430-434

29

436, 445    Jesus is called "Christ" because he is the anointed one, the Messiah. Jesus is also proclaimed as the only Son of God, a title that acknowledges his divinity. After his resurrection, Jesus' divine sonship was manifested in the power of his glorified humanity. Jesus is also called "Lord," another name which acknowledges his divinity.

457-460     The Son of God became a human being in order to bring forgiveness, knowledge of God's love, and a share in divine nature. He also serves as a model of holiness for all people.

464, 470,   Jesus Christ is truly human, with a human mind, will,
480         and body. Jesus Christ is also truly God. His two natures, human and divine, are united in the one person of God's Son.

*Conceived by the power of the Holy Spirit and born of the Virgin Mary (n. 484-570)*

486,        Jesus Christ was conceived of the Virgin Mary by the
491-495     power of the Holy Spirit. Mary was conceived without original sin through the Immaculate Conception, gave her consent to God's Word at the Annunciation, and is truly the Mother of God.

501         Jesus is Mary's only son, but her motherhood includes all those whom Jesus came to save.

516-520     Jesus Christ's entire life reveals God and the mystery of God's redemption. His birth, hidden early life, baptism, temptations, teachings about the kingdom, miraculous signs, and going to Jerusalem to die provide us with a model for truth, service, and holiness.

525, 531    Jesus was born into a poor family. He was a fervent Jew whose life, for the most part, was lived in an ordinary manner working as a manual laborer.

Jesus' public life started with his baptism in the Jordan.     535,
After that Jesus began to proclaim that the Kingdom of   541-547
God was at hand, especially for the poor and for sinners. Jesus' words were accompanied by miracles or
"signs of God's power. "

Jesus chose twelve of his disciples to share his life and   551-553
participate in his mission. He gave them a share in his
authority and sent them to teach and heal. Simon Peter
held first place among the Twelve and was entrusted
with specific authority and leadership.

### Suffering and death (n. 571-630)

Jesus Christ's death and resurrection are the heart of        571
the gospel that is proclaimed to the world.

From the beginning of Jesus' ministry, certain Jewish         574
leaders set out to destroy him. Some leaders were scan-
dalized by his mercy toward sinners. He was thought
by others to be possessed and was eventually accused of
blasphemy and religious crimes punishable by death.

Jesus did not come to abolish the Jewish law, but to          577,
fulfill it. He held deep respect for the temple, and was   583-584
angered at the commercialism in its outer court.

Not all the Jewish leaders agreed with the decision to     597-598
have Jesus executed. Neither the Jews of that era nor
Jews in subsequent times are responsible for Jesus'
death. The personal guilt of those directly responsible
is known only to God. Jesus himself forgave those who
brought about his execution. As sinners, however, we
are all somehow implicated in Jesus' death.

Jesus' death is part of God's mysterious plan of salva-       599,
tion. Jesus took our guilt to himself and in his death   603-604
sacrificed himself for the sins of all human beings

606, 609,   Death on the cross is the culmination of Christ's entire
614, 627    life of giving himself to save others. He accepted his
            suffering and death freely and viewed it as an act of
            love. Jesus' death is a unique sacrifice, which definitive-
            ly redeems all human persons. Jesus' death was a real
            death and put an end to his earthly human existence.

### Resurrection and Ascension (n. 631-682)

638-639,    God's raising of Jesus from the dead was the central
642         belief of the first Christian community. Christ's res-
            urrection is a real event and his appearances as the ris-
            en Lord are the basis for Christian faith.

641-642     Mary Magdalene and the holy women met the risen
            Lord first and became the first to bring the message of
            the resurrection to the apostles. The risen Lord ap-
            peared to Peter and to the Twelve. As witnesses to the
            risen Lord, they form the foundation of the church.

645-647     The risen Lord established direct contact with his dis-
            ciples. Christ's risen body was real, yet glorified and
            not limited to time or space. Resurrection was not a re-
            turn to earthly life, but a passing into another life. The
            resurrection was a transcendent event, and no one wit-
            nessed the actual event.

651-655     Jesus Christ's resurrection confirms all his works and
            teachings and validates his divinity. By his resurrec-
            tion, Christ opens to us the way to resurrected life. The
            risen Christ now lives in the hearts of his disciples who
            hope for the fulfillment of their own resurrection.

668-671     After his final appearance in risen form, Jesus' human-
            ity irrevocably entered into God's glory. He is now the
            master of history and the Lord of the cosmos. Christ is
            present in his church which awaits the fulfillment of
            the kingdom and his final coming in glory.

Jesus Christ did not come to judge, but rather to bring 679
life and salvation. We judge ourselves by either accepting or rejecting God's grace. Thus we receive our
eternal reward according to our works. We can condemn ourselves eternally by rejecting the Spirit of love.

## Commentary

The Catechism places Jesus at the heart of Catholic catechesis
and reminds us that the ultimate aim of all religious instruction
is intimacy with Jesus Christ and his teaching. It also makes note
of the Jewishness of Jesus and the way this has gained emphasis
in contemporary Christology. Not to consider Judaism and the
Torah makes it impossible to understand either Jesus or his mission to reform his own religion. Recent studies about the people
and places that influenced Jesus have helped us understand the
complexities of the Jewish world at the time of Jesus.

Studies in the religious, social, and historical background of
Jesus' time have provided many new insights into the historical
Jesus. While some Protestant biblical scholars find little need to
stress the historical Jesus, Catholic biblical scholars generally
point out the importance of seeing the historical Jesus in continuity with the Christ of faith.

The very nature of the gospels seems to imply that the early
disciples' faith in the resurrection brought them to a profound
awareness of the identity of the risen Lord, and enabled them to
re-interpret the words and deeds of Jesus' public life.

Both the divinity and the humanity of Jesus Christ are foundational to Catholic faith. Traditional church teachings and, to
some extent, the Catechism accentuate the divinity of Christ and
lessen the emphasis given to his full humanity. Today, however,
theologians often present an "ascending theology" which begins
with the historical Jesus, his gradual awareness of his identity,
the growing manifestation of God's power in his life, and the
full validation by God of Jesus' life and mission in his resurrection.

Without overlooking Jesus' divine Sonship and its integral
place in a balanced understanding of Christian beliefs, Jesus' hu-

manity is given special emphasis in contemporary theology. The Letter to the Hebrews tells us that Jesus was like us in all things except sin. This opens up a wide range of considerations about Jesus' inner life and the personal struggles that he had to endure. For many people, this gives the opportunity to identify more closely with Jesus, since he was one of us and knows experientially the joys and sorrows of a human life.

Although Jesus' death and resurrection are the key saving mysteries, we are indeed saved also by all the events of his life. This can link our lives, our work, and our ministry most closely with his. Liberation theology goes beyond the focus of the Catechism when it emphasizes Jesus' preference for the poor, and views him as a liberator who prophetically confronts political and religious oppression and stands in solidarity with the downtrodden.

The Twelve hold special symbolic meaning in the gospels, primarily signifying the new covenant and recalling twelve heads of the ancient tribes of Israel. There is general agreement among biblical scholars about Peter's primacy among the apostles. Also of critical importance for laying the foundation for the church and for the continuation of his ministry, was Jesus' selection of disciples, both women and men, to carry on his mission.

There is no consensus among biblical scholars as to why Jesus was crucified and the Catechism does not attempt to settle this issue. The accounts of Jesus' passion found in the four gospels are stylized dramas, each with its own theological emphasis. We are not sure whether there was actually a trial, nor do we know what the precise charges were. It seems as though the Romans were the only ones who had the authority to execute a person, and so the major blame must be laid with them. Much of the hostility toward the Jews and the fingerpointing for blame might well come from the alienation that Christian communities were feeling toward the Jews in the decades immediately after Jesus' death. Whatever the case, the Catechism points out that only the Jewish leaders who were responsible for Jesus' death can be held accountable. The anti-Semitism that developed out of the notion that Jews are "Christkillers" and which in part helped motivate the Holocaust must be rejected by all Christians.

The Catechism stresses the sacrificial aspect of Jesus' death, wherein he took upon himself our guilt and offered himself to save all people from sin. The church has never formulated an official doctrine of salvation, and thus various interpretations have prevailed over the centuries. For the first thousand years the theory that Jesus ransomed us from the clutches of Satan prevailed. This was replaced by Anselm's (d.1109) "satisfaction theory," which taught that Jesus' death corrected the injustices brought about by our sinful offenses against God. This view prevailed until modern times.

Today salvation is often linked to the ongoing event of creation and viewed as a dynamic process whereby the saving power of God continually "happens" in human experience. It is this process, then, that is revealed and brought to fulfillment in Jesus' death and resurrection.

The Catechism restores the resurrection of Jesus to the central position of faith that it held in the early communities. It is the experience of the risen Lord and the birth of resurrection faith that sparked the beginning of Christianity. When Jesus was raised from the dead, his identity was fully revealed and he was then worshipped as the Christ.

As the Catechism points out, the resurrection validates Jesus' life and his teaching. It was also interpreted by his immediate followers as a pledge of afterlife. The risen Jesus is now the Cosmic Christ who is present in the world, in the church and sacraments, and in the people of all time. Refreshingly, the Catechism reminds us that those who reject him are not judged harshly by Jesus. Rather they condemn themselves by choosing to irrevocably reject the goodness and love that Jesus Christ embodies.

## Suggested Readings

**Jesus**

Fitzmyer, Joseph. *A Christological Catechism*. Mahwah, NJ: Paulist Press, 1982.

Hill, Brennan R. *Jesus the Christ: Contemporary Perspectives*. Mystic, CT: Twenty-Third Publications, 1991.

Johnson, Elizabeth. *Consider Jesus*. New York: Crossroad, 1990.

Lane, Dermot. *Christ at the Centre*. Mahwah, NJ: Paulist Press, 1990.
Sloyan, Gerard. *Jesus in Focus*. Revised edition. Mystic, CT: Twenty-Third Publications, 1994.

# Chapter Three:
# I Believe in the Holy Spirit
### (n. 683-1065)

## Summary

This chapter explains the central teachings about the Holy Spirit, the church, Mary, the forgiveness of sins, the resurrection of the body, and life everlasting. It teaches that one must be touched by the Spirit in order to be in communion with Christ. It is the Spirit who awakens faith and the life of grace. The Spirit has many titles and has been active from the beginning of creation until the present moment. The Spirit was revealed by Jesus who promised to send the Spirit to his followers. The Spirit came on Pentecost, and completes its mission in the church.

The church is the assembly of God's people and the means by which we experience the Spirit today. The church was instituted by Jesus Christ and is the seed and beginning of the kingdom of God on earth. The church is the people of God, the body of Christ. It is one, holy, catholic, and apostolic. The Christian faithful include the hierarchy, those living the consecrated life (priests, Sisters, Brothers), and the laity. The church is also the communion of saints. Mary is the Mother of Christ and the Mother of the church.

The risen Christ conferred on his apostles the power to forgive sins and sent them to proclaim repentance. People who are just will live forever with the risen Lord in heaven after their death. In order to enter heaven, some will undergo purification. Hell is final self-exclusion from communion with God. The last judgment will occur when the Lord returns.

## The Holy Spirit (n. 683-747)

We must first be touched by the Spirit of the Lord in   683-684
order to be united with Jesus Christ. It is the Spirit who
enables us to know God and awakens the faith and the
new life of Christ in each person.

The Spirit is at work throughout God's entire plan for   686, 688
our salvation. The power of the Spirit is experienced in
all aspects of the church: Scripture, Tradition, teaching
authority, liturgy, prayer, ministries, missions, and the
witness of the saints.

Jesus Christ is revealed by the Spirit as the visible im-   689-690
age of the invisible God. When Christ was glorified, he
sent his Spirit to those who believed in him.

The Holy Spirit is called the Paraclete, the Spirit of   692-699
Truth, the Spirit of Christ, the Spirit of God, and many
other titles. The action of the Spirit is symbolized by
water, oil, fire, light, the laying on of hands, and many
other symbols.

The Spirit was active in the beginnings of creation, in   702, 706,
the Hebrew covenant, in the missions of John the   717, 721,
Baptist and the Virgin Mary, and in the life of Jesus   727-737
Christ. At Pentecost the Spirit was given in abundance.
The Spirit's mission is brought to completion in the
church.

## The Catholic Church (n. 748-810)

The church is the assembly of God's people, locally,   751-752
universally, and gathered in liturgy.

Jesus laid the foundation of the church by preaching   763-764,
about the coming of God's kingdom. The kingdom of   766-768
God is manifested in the words, deeds, and presence of

37

Jesus, and then blossoms forth in the church which is the seed and the beginning of the kingdom on earth.

765    Jesus gave the church a structure, particularly in the choice of the twelve apostles with Peter as the leader.

771    The church is a community of faith, hope, and love. It is both visible and spiritual, earthly and heavenly. It is a complex reality with both human and divine elements.

775    The church is a kind of sacrament or sign of God's plan to save all of humanity.

782    All who become God's people through faith and baptism share in Christ's priestly, prophetic, and kingly office.

787-791    The church is the body of Christ. He promised to remain with his people in the church until the end of time, and to send them the Spirit and the Spirit's many special gifts.

*One, holy, catholic, and apostolic (n. 811-870)*

813-815    The church is one in that it comes from the One God and One Lord. It shares one faith, a common celebration of worship and the sacraments, and the recognition of apostolic succession.

817, 821    The church has experienced many divisions, but it constantly seeks to recover unity through renewal, conversion, prayer in common, dialogue, and collaboration.

824, 827    The church is holy because it is united with Christ. All of its members are sinners who must seek to attain holiness through love, penance, and renewal.

830-834    The church is catholic (universal) because Jesus is totally present in it and because it has a mission to the whole human race. The church of Christ is present in all lawful local congregations. Dioceses are Catholic through their communion with the church of Rome, which presides in love.

Those are fully incorporated in the church who accept the entire structure, all the means of salvation it offers, and governance by the pope and bishops. Christians who are baptized but who do not profess the faith entirely have an imperfect communion with the church. The church is linked with the people of Jewish faith by virtue of the common heritage and covenant relationship described in the Hebrew Scriptures. The church also acknowledges its bonds with other religions. 837-842

All salvation comes from Christ through the church. Salvation can be attained by those who sincerely seek God and endeavor to do God's will as recognized by their conscience. 846-847

The church has a mission from Christ to spread the good news of God's salvation to all. The Spirit guides the church in this mission. 849, 852

The church is apostolic because it was founded on the apostles, the witnesses chosen and sent by Christ to spread the message of salvation. Christ is the source and origin of this mission. The task of guarding and communicating the apostolic teaching is now entrusted to the successors of the apostles, the college of bishops. By their baptism, all members of the church share in this mission of spreading the good news. 857, 862, 863-864

*Hierarchy, laity, and consecrated life (n. 871-962)*

There is a genuine equality of dignity and action among all Christ's faithful who carry out his mission. 872

880      Christ appointed the Twelve as a permanent college over which he placed Peter. In a similar way the bishops of today operate under the primacy of the pope.

882-884    The pope, the bishop of Rome and Peter's successor, is the visible basis of unity for the bishops and all the faithful. The pope has full, supreme, and universal power, which he freely exercises over the church. The college of bishops also has such power, but may only exercise it when they are united with the pope or when they are participating in an ecumenical council.

886-887    Individual bishops are the visible basis of unity in their own dioceses. They exercise pastoral authority over the people entrusted to them and share in the pastoral care of all the churches in the diocese. National groups of bishops are called episcopal conferences. Their meetings and pronouncements can make valuable contributions to the spirit of collegiality among the bishops within a country.

888      Bishops, along with their co-worker priests, are authentic teachers of the faith who teach with Christ's authority.

891      Christ shared his own infallibility with his church to preserve the faith. The pope, by virtue of his office, enjoys the charism of infallibility when he definitively proclaims a doctrine of faith or morals. Infallibility also resides with the body of bishops when it exercises its teaching office with the pope, especially in an ecumenical council.

894-895    Bishops govern their dioceses through advice, persuasion, example, authority, and sacred power. Bishops have their own proper authority, but this must be exercised in communion with the whole church and under the leadership of the pope.

| | |
|---|---|
| The laity are called to promote the kingdom in temporal affairs and to be a Christian leaven in social, political, and economic matters. They are entrusted by God through their baptism and confirmation to bring the message of salvation to the world and to share in Christ's prophetic mission. They also can be called upon to work with their pastors and use their gifts in the service of the church community in a variety of ministries. | 898-900, 905, 910 |

Those in the religious state profess to follow the call of poverty, chastity, and obedience in a recognized and stable life consecrated to God. This is one way of experiencing a more intimate consecration to God, one that is grounded in baptism and dedicated totally to God.     915-916, 931

The Communion of Saints includes those who are pilgrims on earth, the dead who are being purified, and the blessed in heaven. Prayers can be offered for the dead, and the saints can intercede with God for us.     954, 958

*Mary, Mother of Christ and the Church, forgiveness, resurrection, and life everlasting (n. 963-1065)*

Mary is the Mother of Christ and of the church. She is the model of faith and love. Taken body and soul into heaven at the end of her life, she now cooperates in an unparalleled way in the work of the Savior.     963, 966-968

Mary is a sign of hope and comfort for God's pilgrim people. Devotion to the Virgin Mary is intrinsic to Christian worship. It can also foster worship of the triune God.     968, 971-972

When the risen Christ gave the Spirit to his apostles, he conferred on them his own divine power to forgive sins.     976

977        Jesus Christ connected the forgiveness of sins to faith
           and baptism. Baptism, the first and chief sacrament of
           forgiveness, joins us to Christ who died for our sins
           and justified us in his resurrection.

979        The church must be able to forgive all penitents their
           sins, even to the last moment of their lives.

980-982    The baptized can be reconciled with God and with the
           church through the sacrament of penance. The church
           can forgive any offense, no matter how serious.

989        Christ is truly risen from the dead and lives forever.
           After death the righteous will live forever with the ris-
           en Christ. He will raise them up on the last day.

991        Belief in the resurrection of the dead has always been
           an essential element of the Christian faith.

995        Experience of the risen Christ is linked to the Christian
           hope of resurrection. To be a witness to Christ is to be
           a witness to his resurrection.

999-1000   Christ will transform our earthly bodies into spiritual
           bodies. The "how" of resurrection goes beyond our
           imagination and understanding. It is accessible only
           through faith.

1002       Christ will raise us up on the last day. In a way, we are
           already risen with him. Christian life already shares in
           Christ's death and resurrection.

1007       Death comes as the normal end of life and gives a
           sense of urgency to our life. We have only a limited
           time to fulfill our destiny.

1009,      Christ has transformed death. Jesus took our death
1020       upon himself in obedience to his Father's will.

Christians unite their own death to Jesus' death. They view death as the final step toward Christ and everlasting life.

The New Testament refers to judgment primarily as the final encounter with Christ in his second coming. Scripture also frequently says that each person will be rewarded according to his or her works and faith immediately after death.                    1021

People who die in God's grace and friendship and are perfectly purified will live forever with Christ. They will see God face to face.                    1023

Heaven is the ultimate fulfillment of humanity's deepest longing. It is the state of supreme and final happiness. This mystery of blessed union with God and with those who are in Christ is beyond all description and comprehension.                    1024-27

All who die in God's grace and friendship are assured of eternal salvation. Those not yet perfectly purified need purification after death.                    1030

The church has always honored the memory of the dead and offered prayers, especially the eucharistic sacrifice of the Mass, for them. The church prays that the dead may gain the beatific vision of God.                    1032

We can be united with God only if we freely choose to love God. We deny God's love if we sin gravely. Jesus warns us that we shall be separated from him if we fail to meet the serious needs of the poor and the little ones. Hell is the state of final self-exclusion from union with God and the blessed ones.                    1033

The last judgment will come when Christ returns in glory. Then we shall realize the ultimate meaning of                    1040 the whole work of creation. At the end of time the kingdom of God will be fulfilled, and there will be a definitive realization of God's plan to gather all things into one in Christ.

## Commentary

The Catechism reclaims a treasured theology of the Holy Spirit. The Spirit is viewed as having been active in creation. The presence of the Spirit in the covenants formed with Abraham, Moses, and the other leaders of the Hebrew Scriptures as well as in the missions of John the Baptist, Mary, and the church is also highlighted. Many theologians today go beyond this to point out the inclusive presence of the Spirit in the cosmos, as well as in all cultures and religions.

The discussion of the church opens with the Second Vatican Council's emphasis on the church as the assembly of God's people, a community of disciples, and the sacrament of God's salvation for all people. The traditional notion of Jesus founding a church is nuanced with the observation that Jesus laid a foundation for the church by preaching about the coming of the kingdom of God.

Many theologians point out the important distinction between the kingdom and the church. Rather than being identified with the kingdom, the church is a sign of its presence and is called to promote the coming of God's kingdom. Here and previously throughout the Catechism another neglected belief is stressed—that through baptism and faith all Christians share with Christ in his role as priest, prophet, and king. Many of the faithful are not aware of this identity, nor of their rights and responsibilities to participate in the life and ministry of the church.

Unity has been an ideal for the church since its beginning. It was the object of Jesus' own prayer in the Gospel of John. While Christianity holds sacred the oneness of its faith and its community, it has been marked by serious divisions from its beginnings. The most serious divisions were East from West in the eleventh century and Protestant from Catholic in the sixteenth century. The Second Vatican Council did a great deal to heal these divisions. Following the Council, many dialogues were carried out among the churches, along with symbolic gestures of reconciliation. Many ecumenists point out that the movement toward unity has stalled in recent years. They point out that the common ground that has been established in dialogue needs now to be translated into practice, especially in the areas of Eucharistic sharing (intercommunion) and the recognition of ministry.

A major insight of Vatican II was that *all* of Jesus' disciples, not only the clergy and religious Sisters and Brothers, are called to holiness. It is important to point out that the only source of holiness is God alone, and that the church's holiness flows from its union with Jesus Christ. In view of this universal call to holiness, it seems that there is now a need to develop spiritualities suitable for the vast numbers of laity who work and struggle in the everyday world.

Many think that a spiritual vacuum was created when devotional spirituality, characterized by the Rosary, novenas, and benediction, was set aside after the Second Vatican Council and not replaced. To fill the void, some of the faithful are returning to traditional forms of piety and devotional spirituality while others seek to give their lives a spiritual dimension by using Eastern or other eclectic practices of prayer and meditation, or by finding God's peaceful presence and a spirit of community in self-help and recovery groups.

The Catechism describes Catholicity as Jesus' universal presence in the church as well as the church's mission to all the world. In the past, "world church" often meant the presence of the European church throughout the world, a presence that was often perceived by indigenous people as being colonial. Today "world church" is coming to mean the presence of the church in many cultures, nourishing each culture and adapting the traditional church structures and message to the local needs and customs.

The language of "outside the church there is no salvation" has been replaced. The Catechism acknowledges that salvation is possible for all who sincerely seek God and follow their conscience in trying to do God's will. Even though salvation ultimately comes through Christ and the church, it needs to be recognized and stated more clearly that for most people salvation is achieved in other churches, other religions, and outside of organized religion altogether.

The church is apostolic in that it is true to the message of Jesus as taught to the apostles. Its apostolic mission to spread the gospel must also be respectful of religious freedom and the integrity of the religions it encounters in its missions. The constraints of space allowed only the briefest mention of this topic in the Catechism. A great deal more education about other religions needs to be provided for Catholics.

In keeping with the Vatican II perspective, the text acknowledges the equality and dignity of all Christ's disciples. In this context the Catechism then explains the various offices that serve the community of believers. The ongoing struggle to shift from a "church of unequals" to a "church of equals" is of major importance in renewing the structures and the exercise of authority in the church.

The Catechism draws a parallel between Jesus' appointment of the Twelve as a permanent college over which he placed Peter as the head and the existing hierarchic structure of bishops and the pope. The limitations of this parallel can be seen in the analysis provided by contemporary biblical studies and historical theology. For example, the word "Apostle" in the New Testament sometimes refers to the Twelve and at other times more broadly refers to the missionaries of the church. The designation of "The Twelve" seems to be a symbolic reference to the heads of the ancient twelve tribes of Israel more than a definitive head count of Jesus' closest followers. There is a strong consensus, among both Catholics and Protestants, that Jesus gave Peter a position of primacy among the Twelve. The original Twelve, however, were never replaced. Although Matthias was elected to fill the spot left vacant by Judas's betrayal of Christ, the original Twelve were not replaced as they died. With the exception of Peter, we know little if anything about the ministry of these original twelve apostles in the early church.

Many theologians today maintain that apostolic succession does not refer to an unbroken line of officials going back to the apostles. Rather, they understand it as a way of seeing the teachings of the present church in continuity with the teachings that Jesus handed on to the original apostles.

The identification of the pope as Peter's successor also needs to be put into historical context. There is a broad consensus among biblical scholars that Jesus gave Peter a primary place among the apostles. At the same time there is the awareness that the position of the Bishop of Rome only gradually gained primacy over the other bishops. By the fourth century the Bishops of Rome explicitly claimed to be the successors of Peter. It was Pope Leo I (d. 461) who drew together patristic references to the primacy of Peter and formulated the Roman office of the papacy, tracing it from Jesus to Peter to the Bishop of Rome.

The papacy continued to go through various stages of evolution, moving from the Roman-type of authority in the Post-Constantinian church to a feudal structure in the Middle Ages. With the rise of nation states in the fourteenth and fifteenth centuries, more markedly political models of the papacy began to appear.

It was not until the First Vatican Council in 1870, at a time when the position of the papacy was being severely challenged in Europe, that the papacy was bolstered with a strong definition regarding the supreme power and infallible authority of the pope in matters of faith and morals. The Second Vatican Council reaffirmed this teaching, but tried to establish a balance of power by acknowledging that the authority which bishops receive at their episcopal ordination is the same as the authority of the pope when it is exercised along with him. The Second Vatican Council itself modeled a collegial and consultative style of authority which signaled a new direction in the way church leaders carried out their responsibilities of leadership. Tensions arise at all levels of the church today when some church leaders return to a more authoritarian style of leadership.

Vatican II's emphasis on the collegial authority of the bishops also had its impact on priests and the laity. Now aware of their identity as the people of God in a "church of equals," many lay Catholics wish to participate in the decision-making process of the church. This has moved many church leaders and communities to a more consultative way of making decisions

Moreover, many bishops and priests now choose to lead through inspiration and persuasion rather than through edict. The episcopal conference in the United States has effectively used its authority on several occasions to teach its people and, indeed, the nation by presenting the Catholic perspective on nuclear disarmament, economic justice, and other issues.

Papal infallibility, as defined by Vatican I in 1870, is often misunderstood by those inside and outside the church. The Catechism describes infallibility as a charism which Christ gave his church, and which is exercised by the pope only when he definitively proclaims a doctrine of faith or morals by virtue of his office. Since the definition in 1870, only one pope has exercised the charism of infallibility: Pius XII in 1950 when he defined the dogma of Mary's Assumption.

The Catechism considers Mary in the context of her relationship with Jesus and with the church. This contemporary approach to the mother of Jesus does not use the terms of the more traditional patronage model, but rather concentrates on Mary's solidarity with all disciples of Jesus. She stands as a woman who is a model of faith, the epitome of how "amazing grace" can work in a person's life. Liberation theology has viewed Mary as a woman strongly confronting injustice and oppression, as is evidenced in her Magnificat. Feminist theologians have found in Mary a model of courage and determination to be faithful to God's calling in a world where women are oppressed.

As Part One of the Catechism continues its explanation of the Creed, the topic shifts to forgiveness. This chapter professes Jesus' power to forgive sins and explains how the church has been commissioned to exercise this power, especially in the sacraments of baptism and penance. This topic will receive more detailed treatment in Part Two when the Catechism considers the sacraments of healing.

The final portion of this section deals with the traditional four last things: death, judgment, heaven, and hell. For the disciple of Jesus, death draws hope and meaning from the resurrection. Since heaven is an experience of union with God that is beyond description and understanding, little can be said about it other than that it is the ultimate goal of all believers.

The Catechism also reiterates the traditional belief that there is some purification after death, and that the church believes in the efficacy of praying for the dead. The traditional term of "purgatory" is maintained. Surprisingly, the purification of "cleansing fire" is still mentioned, although it is acknowledged to be an image. Belief in hell is professed, but not in terms of condemnation to a place of torture, but rather as self-exclusion from union with God. Throughout the text condemnatory judgment by God is replaced by the human free choice for evil.

Contemporary eschatology often shifts from the four last things to a consideration of the kingdom, both as realized today and in the age to come. There is an attempt to put our life and our daily struggles for freedom and growth into harmony with the ultimate fulfillment of God's saving plan. There is also a call to bring peace and order to the world and thus open it to the coming of God's reign.

## Suggested Readings

**Holy Spirit**
Burns, J. Patout, and Gerald Fagin. *The Holy Spirit*. Collegeville, MN: Liturgical Press (Glazier Books), 1984.

**Church**
Chittister, Joan, *Womanstrength: Modern Church, Modern Women*. Kansas City: Sheed and Ward, 1990.
Doyle, Dennis M. *The Church Emerging from Vatican II*. Mystic, CT: Twenty-Third Publications, 1992.
Schillebeeckx, Edward. *Church: The Human Story of God*. New York: Crossroad, 1990.

**Mary**
Brown, Raymond, et al. *Mary in the New Testament*. Mahwah, NJ: Paulist Press, 1978.

**Eschatology**
Galvin, John, ed. *Faith and the Future: Studies in Christian Eschatology*. Mahwah, NJ: Paulist Press, 1993.

# PART TWO

# THE CELEBRATION OF THE CHRISTIAN MYSTERY

# Part Two:
# The Celebration of the
# Christian Mystery

### Summary

Part Two presents the celebration of the mysteries of Christ's life as expressed in the liturgical worship that is central to the church and the life of its members. The first section discusses the paschal mystery, the sacraments in general, and the celebration of the paschal mystery. Section Two explains the seven sacraments. The treatment of the liturgy begins with a discussion of the "why" and "what" of liturgy, and explains why catechesis on the liturgy is important. The liturgy is described as the "work" of God, Christ, and the church. It is the commemoration of God's saving work in history and the celebration of the mysteries of Christ's life. These mysteries form the foundation of the seven sacraments that are celebrated by the church. The purpose of the sacraments is to help people toward holiness and to express worship to God. The sacraments confer grace by the power of God.

Liturgy is celebrated by the whole community, although not all members have the same function. Liturgy is celebrated through signs, symbols, words, actions, singing, and music. These celebrations occur in various forms throughout the liturgical year.

# Section One:
# The Sacramental Economy

*Why liturgy?* (n. 1066-1076)

Christ completed the task of redeeming humanity through the paschal mystery which consists of his blessed passion, resurrection, and ascension. Liturgy celebrates the paschal mystery through which Christ saves us.

1067

Christ continues the work of our redemption in the liturgy of the church. The liturgy is the summit toward which all the activity of the church is directed; it is the font from which all the church's power flows.

1069,
1074

# Chapter One:
# The Paschal Mystery
## (n. 1077-1134)

Christ makes his paschal mystery present through the church's liturgy. Christ is always present to his church, especially in its liturgical celebrations.

1085,
1088

In the "today" of its liturgy the church relives the great events of salvation. Christian liturgy not only recalls the events that saved us but also makes them present and real today.

1095,
1104

1097,      Every liturgical action, especially the celebration of the
1108       eucharist and the sacraments, is an encounter between
           Christ and the church. The Holy Spirit is sent to us in
           every liturgical action to bring us into communion
           with Christ and so to form his body.

1115,      The mysteries of Christ's life are the foundation for the
1117       sacraments. The church has gradually recognized the
           treasures of Christ and over the centuries has discerned
           that there are seven sacraments instituted by Christ.

1119,      The church acts in the sacraments as a priestly com-
1120-21    munity. The priestly people are prepared by baptism
           and confirmation to celebrate the eucharistic liturgy.
           Those consecrated through the sacrament of ordination
           serve the church in the name of Christ. Those ordained
           to the ministerial priesthood serve those who possess
           the priesthood of the baptized.

1123,      The purpose of the sacraments is to make people holy,
1127       build up the Body of Christ, and offer worship to God.
           The sacraments confer the grace that they signify if
           they are celebrated in faith. This sacramental grace is
           the grace of the Holy Spirit.

# Chapter Two:
# The Celebration
# of the Paschal Mystery
### (n. 1135-1209)

1140-43    The entire community celebrates sacramental liturgy.
           The celebrating assembly is the community of the bap-
           tized, consecrated to a common priesthood—the priest-
           hood of Christ. Not all members of the assembly have
           the same function. Some are consecrated by the sacra-

ment of holy orders; others are not ordained but perform particular liturgical and pastoral ministries.

A sacramental celebration includes signs and symbols. God speaks to us through visible creation. These realities can embody God's sanctifying action as well as the human action of offering worship to God.

1145, 1148

The sacraments purify and integrate all the rich signs and symbols of the cosmos and human social life.

1152

The Liturgy of the Word is integral to all sacramental celebrations. God's word is to be presented in a fitting manner so that it can nourish the faith of the believers.

1154

Music and singing fulfill their function in the celebration when they express the beauty of prayer, the participation of the community, and the solemnity of the celebration.

1157

The particular events of the one paschal mystery unfold in the course of the liturgical year. The sanctoral cycle of feast days honors Mary, the martyrs, and the saints.

1171

The worship of the church is not bound exclusively to any one place. The whole earth is sacred and has been entrusted to us. Church buildings are houses of prayer and gathering places that signify and reveal the church living in a particular place.

1179-80

The liturgy is carried out in a variety of forms that reflect the diverse cultures of all people. Christ's mystery is so rich that no one liturgical tradition can exhaust its expression.

1200-01

Christ is revealed to particular peoples and cultures through the liturgical life of a given church. The

1202-06

church's catholicity enables it to purify and gather into its own unity the true riches of all cultures. Liturgical diversity can be a source of enrichment. This diversity, however, must not damage church unity.

## Commentary

This section follows the Second Vatican Council perspective that links liturgy and the sacraments with Jesus Christ and the saving mysteries of his life. Liturgy makes these mysteries present and celebrates them. The reclamation of the theology of the Risen Lord and his Spirit has enabled the church to understand more clearly the significance and centrality of the liturgy and the sacraments. It is Jesus Christ who is the primary priest, celebrant, and point of focus for all liturgy and worship.

Liturgy and sacraments are viewed as dynamic encounters between the people of God and Jesus Christ, a perspective which owes much to the work of Edward Schillebeeckx, a Dutch Dominican theologian. This is a more relational and communal approach to liturgy and sacraments than some of the more legalistic and cleric-centered views of the past.

"Institution by Christ" is understood differently today, now that the church recognizes the contribution of biblical criticism and historical studies. We now realize that the church's rituals and sacraments have all undergone change and development with the passage of time. From this point of view, one might say that the church and the Spirit of the Lord are co-authors of liturgy and sacraments. In effect, many theologians hold that the sacraments have been instituted by the church under the inspiration of Jesus Christ.

The Catechism consistently emphasizes the priesthood of all believers, thereby endorsing a belief that had been rather neglected from the Council of Trent until Vatican II. It explains that the ordained priesthood is charged with serving the needs of the priesthood of the faithful while the latter group is reminded to become more involved in the liturgy. The laity's role in collaborating with the priest needs to be stressed even more since far too many Catholics assume the role of spectator, rather than participating partner.

Thanks to the work of twentieth-century theologians like Jesuits Piet Franzen and Karl Rahner, the church has a richer theology of grace. In the past, grace was often objectified and even measured. Now it is viewed as a dynamic sharing in the very life of God, and so, the phrase "to confer grace" should be understood in this context.

Henri de Lubac, a French Jesuit theologian, challenged the split-level world of natural and supernatural. He preferred to view reality as a unified whole in which creation is graced by the very fact that it comes from God. Humans are similarly graced because they are created in God's image.

Faith is essential to the celebration of the sacraments. In explaining this, the Catechism moves beyond the view that it is sufficient merely "not to place obstacles in the way" of receiving sacraments. If sacraments are true encounters with the Lord, a holistic faith response, not a mere passive reception, is required. Ongoing educational and pastoral effort is needed to move many Catholics beyond a passive and, at times, "magical" attitude toward ritual and sacraments.

The Catechism's basic presentation can be enriched by a review of the importance of symbols in rituals and the sacraments. The human sciences of linguistics, literary criticism, psychology, communication arts, and the history of religions provide valuable insights into the nature and meaning of religious symbols. Phenomenology draws attention to the importance of "meaning" in our rituals. This is especially important when we realize that many Catholics, especially the young, have lost touch with the significance and the power of rituals and sacraments. The secularization of life and culture has caused many people to lose the sense of transcendence and awe before the holy that is integral to proper worship. Sacramental celebrations should lift people beyond the mundane and the trivial, and at the same time be relevant to everyday life. Catholics struggle to maintain this balance. Growth will come only by taking the basic principles stated in the Catechism and giving them meaning in a pastoral context.

Catholic thinkers like Rahner and the Jesuit paleontologist-theologian Teilhard de Chardin have made us aware that the world is indeed sacramental. In daily life there is a liturgy of the world, a "Mass on the world." Everyday life is integrally linked with liturgy. This perspective, while not mentioned in the Catechism, is especially useful in Catholic efforts to integrate our religious tradition with contemporary efforts to save and sustain the environment.

Words are also used as symbols. Awareness of the power of language helps people see the "Word" of scripture as a dynamic way to encounter the Risen Lord. Consequently, scripture has been restored to a central role in liturgy and the sacraments. This scriptural emphasis has moved contemporary Catholicism closer to the practice of the early communities, and also brought it into greater harmony with the Protestant traditions.

The importance of culture and liturgical diversity is recognized in the Catechism. We have moved, as Rahner points out, to become a "world church." The colonial period, which saw domination by Western European culture, seems to be ending. In the post-Vatican II period there is a new respect for indigenous peoples and the value of culture. Liturgy can profitably draw from culture as well as play an important role in transforming culture.

## Suggested Readings

**Liturgy**

Collins, Mary. *Worship: Renewal to Practice.* Washington, DC: Pastoral Press, 1987.

Downey, Michael, and Richard Fragomeni, eds. *A Promise of Presence.* Washington, DC: Pastoral Press, 1992.

Empereur, James. *Worship: Exploring the Sacred.* Washington, DC: Pastoral Press, 1987.

Kilmartin, Edward J. *Christian Liturgy: I. Theology.* Kansas City: Sheed and Ward, 1988.

**Sacraments**

Huebsch, Bill. *Rethinking the Sacraments.* Mystic, CT: Twenty-Third Publications, 1989.

Osborne, Kenan B. *Sacramental Theology.* Mahwah, NJ: Paulist Press, 1988.

# Section Two:
# The Seven Sacraments

## Chapter One:
## The Sacraments of Initiation
### (n. 1210-1419)

### Summary

This chapter explains the three sacraments of initiation: baptism, confirmation, and eucharist. Baptism is the basis of the Christian life. It frees people from sin and incorporates them into the church. Christian initiation comes about in several stages and has certain essential elements. The catechumenate is important for preparing adults for baptism. Infant baptism should be conferred shortly after birth. Faith is required for baptism. Salvation is linked to the sacrament of baptism, but God's saving power is not bound to the sacraments. Baptism forgives sins and brings about a new birth in the Spirit and incorporates people into the church.

Confirmation completes baptism. By this sacramental anointing the confirmed are sealed with the Spirit. Confirmation has a number of effects; therefore, those being confirmed should receive proper preparation.

Eucharist completes Christian initiation. It is the source and summit of the church's life. The eucharist was instituted by Jesus Christ and has been celebrated from the beginning of the church. The celebration of the Mass unfolds according to a structured movement. It is a memorial of Christ's Passover and a sacrifice. Christ's presence in the eucharist is unique and real, and is worshipped both during the Mass and at other times. The celebration of the eucharist is directed toward the reception of Christ's body in communion.

## Baptism (n. 1210-1284)

1213    Baptism frees people from sin, gives them rebirth as God's children, incorporates them into Christ's church, and grants them a share in his mission.

1229    Becoming a Christian is accomplished by a personal faith journey and a multi-stage initiation. The essential elements of initiation are: proclamation of the word, acceptance of the gospel, conversion, profession of faith, baptism, the outpouring of the Spirit, and access to the eucharist.

1247-48    The catechumenate is important for adult initiation. The catechumenate fosters conversion and formation so that the catechumen is properly disposed to accept God's gift in the sacraments of initiation.

1250,    Infant baptism witnesses to the pure, unmerited gift of
1261    the grace of salvation, and should be conferred shortly after birth. The church trusts in God's mercy toward children who have died without baptism.

1253-55    Faith is required for baptism; not necessarily a perfect or mature faith, but one that is initial and open to increase. Parents, sponsors, and the whole church community bear responsibility for the development and protection of baptismal grace.

1257    Baptism is necessary for salvation for those who have heard the gospel proclaimed and have the possibility of asking for the sacrament. God has linked salvation to baptism, but God is not bound to the sacraments.

1260    Those who are ignorant of the gospel and the church, but who seek the truth and do God's will as they understand it, can be saved.

## *Confirmation* (n. 1285-1321)

Confirmation binds the baptized more closely to the church, confers special strength from the Spirit, and more strictly obliges confirmed Christians to be true witnesses to Christ.    1285

Confirmation is conferred through the anointing with chrism, the laying on of hands, and the words: "Be sealed with the gift of the Holy Spirit." The rite concludes with the bishop giving the sign of peace.    1300-01

Confirmation completes baptism. It unites Christians more closely with the Father, Son, and Spirit, and with the church, and gives them special power to spread and defend the faith.    1303-05

Catechesis for confirmation should awaken a sense of belonging to both the universal church and the parish community. The latter bears the responsibility of preparing the candidates for confirmation.    1309

## *Eucharist* (n. 1322-1419)

The eucharist is the source and summit of the Christian life. It is an action of thanksgiving to God, a re-enactment of the last supper, and a memorial of the Lord's passion and resurrection.    1324, 1328-29

At the heart of the eucharistic celebration is the bread and wine which become the body and blood of Christ by the words of Christ and the invocation of the Spirit.    1333

Jesus instituted the eucharist as a memorial of his death and resurrection. He commanded his apostles to celebrate the eucharist, thereby making them "priests of the new covenant."    1337

1348-55    The Mass unfolds according to a structure consisting of the gathering, the Liturgy of the Word, and the Liturgy of the Eucharist.

1358-59    The celebration of the eucharist is an offering of praise and thanksgiving for the work of creation. In this sacrifice the whole of creation is presented to God through the death and resurrection of Christ.

1363-65    The biblical notion of "memorial" both recalls past events and proclaims in the present the marvels God has done. In the liturgy these events become present and actual. The eucharist remembers and re-presents Christ's passover.

1367       The eucharist is a sacrifice in that Christ gives again the same body that suffered on the cross and the same blood that was shed.

1374       The mode of Christ's presence in the eucharist is unique. It is called "the real presence." This is not meant in an exclusive way, as if his other modes of being present are not real. This presence is real par excellence, since Christ, God and man, becomes present.

1378       The Catholic Church continues to worship the real presence of Christ in the eucharist during Mass, as well as reserved in the tabernacle outside the celebration of the Mass.

1382       The celebration of the eucharistic liturgy is wholly directed toward the intimate union of the faithful with Christ through the reception of Christ's body and blood in communion.

1393       The eucharist, in uniting believers to Christ, cleanses them from past sins and preserves them from future sins.

The eucharist directs the church's concern toward the     1397
poor. To receive mindfully the body and blood of
Christ, people should recognize Christ in the poorest
of his brothers and sisters.

## Commentary

Although the Catechism connects baptism with freedom from
sin, there is not the former emphasis on the removal of original
sin. In fact, the biblical notion of baptism centers on being
plunged into the mysteries of Christ and intitiated into his
church. Original sin is a later notion that is not constitutive of the
theology of baptism.

The catechumenate is rapidly becoming one of the most effective processes in today's church. The ancient way of initiating
new members has been restored, and has brought enormous
spiritual and formational benefits to inquirers and candidates as
well as sponsors. In the initiation rite for the catechumenate the
original sequence of baptism, confirmation, and eucharist has
been restored.

There is no mention in the Catechism of limbo as the place of
repose for infants who die unbaptized. While it advises trusting
in God's mercy to save unbaptized infants, the Catechism also
expresses a sense of urgency about having infants baptized, but
does not give any explanation for this.

Contemporary pastoral practice generally requires some assurance that the child to be baptized will be raised Catholic. The
occasion of an infant baptism is generally an opportune moment
to catechize the parents and ascertain the depth of their faith.
Since the Catechism states clearly that faith is required in the reception of all sacraments, theologians will continue to discuss
how faith is operative in infant baptism.

The Catechism maintains that baptism is necessary for salvation, yet it acknowledges that salvation is also accessible for
those who are not baptized. One of the major breakthroughs of
Vatican II was the recognition that those who seek the truth and
do God's will can be saved. The older and difficult-to-explain
phrase "outside the church there is no salvation" is not used in
the Catechism's discussion of salvation.

The centrality of the Spirit of Christ and the ecclesial dimension of confirmation have been restored to the theological understanding of this sacrament. The renewal of confirmation also links it closely with baptism and eucharist, following the more ancient tradition of initiation.

In recent times religious educators and pastoral leaders have spent a great amount of effort preparing the young for confirmation. It is also vital to prepare the parents, sponsors, and the parish itself for the celebration of this sacrament. Offering young people a sense of hospitality and caring is viewed by many as an essential context for this sacrament.

The "age" question remains largely unresolved in the Catechism. It uses the same words that are used in the Code of Canon Law and recommends the "age of discernment" as the appropriate time for confirmation. Some liturgists and theologians hold for a younger age, so that the sequence of the initiation rites of baptism, confirmation, and eucharist is observed. Others prefer to delay the sacrament, so that it can reflect a more mature choice on the part of the candidate. Theology seems to be adjusted to whatever age is chosen, and it is unlikely that this matter will be clarified or resolved for some time to come.

The eucharist is described as a liturgical action and a memorial meal wherein Jesus Christ is really present. The Catechism refrains from putting "institution by Christ" and the priesthood of the apostles into a historical context. Biblical criticism has given Catholics access to rich insights into the varying accounts of eucharist in the New Testament. These scriptural accounts reflect not only the historical actions of Jesus, but also the various liturgical traditions in the early house churches. The celebration of the eucharist seems to have been a post-resurrection ritual. The presiders over these early liturgies were probably the leaders of the communities. Ordained priesthood does not seem to appear until the second century and does not seem to have been associated with Jesus' apostles.

The sacrificial element of eucharist might be better nuanced, with particular sensitivity to ecumenical dialogue. Phrases like "unbloody sacrifice" or "reenactment" appear in the Catechism despite their being open to misunderstanding. The Catechism summarizes the traditional understanding of the sacrifice at Calvary as a one-time event with complete redemptive power. At the same time, the Risen Lord personally continues this sacrifice in the eucharist. Christ is the sacrifice, and where Christ is, his self-offering is made present.

The real presence is best understood in terms of the presence of the Risen Lord. It is real and yet spiritual. How this takes place is not so much the focus of contemporary theology. Rather, contemporary thinkers ponder the meaning and power that is available through Christ's presence.

Biblical criticism on the table ministry of Jesus and on the feeding miracles links the eucharist with his ministry to the poor and the outcast. Liberation theology highlights the prophetic dimensions of eucharist, and explains that communion, the goal of eucharist, includes communion and solidarity with the starving and the oppressed.

### Suggested Readings

Austin, Gerard. *Anointing with the Spirit: The Rite of Confirmation.* Collegeville, MN: Liturgical Press (Pueblo Books), 1985.

Bourgeois, Henry. *On Becoming Christian: Christian Initiation and Its Sacraments.* Mystic, CT: Twenty-Third Publications, 1984.

Hellwig, Monika. *The Eucharist and the Hunger of the World.* Revised edition. Kansas City: Sheed and Ward, 1993.

Osborne, Kenan B. *The Christian Sacraments of Initiation.* Mahwah, NJ: Paulist Press, 1987.

Turner, Paul. *Confirmation.* Mahwah, NJ: Paulist Press, 1993.

# Chapter Two:
# Sacraments of Healing
## (n. 1420-1532)

### Summary

This chapter discusses the sacraments of reconciliation and the anointing of the sick. The sacrament of reconciliation is also called penance, confession, and the sacrament of pardon or forgiveness. In this sacrament Jesus summons people to inner conversion. Conversion is accomplished in many ways. The sacrament includes acts of the individual and the action of God. The acts of the penitent are contrition, confession, and satisfaction. Acting in the person of Christ, bishops and priests exercise the ministry of reconciliation through absolution. The effects of this sacrament are forgiveness of sin and reconciliation with the church. This sacrament can be celebrated individually or communally.

The anointing of the sick recalls Jesus' compassion for the sick and the many healings he performed. In this sacrament the church carries out the Lord's ministry to the sick. Jesus gave suffering a redemptive meaning and he calls all people to do the same. This sacrament is for those who are in danger of death or who are dying. It is administered through an anointing in a liturgical celebration. This sacrament comforts the sick, unites them to Christ's passion, allows them to contribute to the sanctification of the church, and prepares them for death.

### Penance and Reconciliation (n. 1420-1498)

1424  This sacrament recognizes and praises God's holiness and mercy toward sinful humanity. It imparts the love of the reconciling God to the sinner.

1427-28, Jesus summons all people to conversion as part of his
1431  proclamation of the kingdom. He calls them to a conversion of heart, a radical reorientation of their lives.

1435  Conversion is accomplished in daily life by gestures of reconciliation, care of the poor, concern for justice, admission of offenses, correction, amendment, examination of conscience, spiritual direction, and taking up one's cross daily.

1440  Sin is an offense against God, a rupture of a person's communion with God. At the same time, sin harms a person's communion with the church.

Only God can forgive sin. Jesus, by virtue of his divine            1441
authority, gives this power to human beings to ex-
ercise in his name.

Jesus forgave sins during his public life and restored         1443-46
sinners into the community of God's people. Christ instituted the sacrament of penance for all sinful members of the church.

The fundamental structure of the sacrament remains in            1448
place despite the changes which this sacrament has undergone over the centuries. The two essential elements
are acts of the penitent and the action of the Spirit.

The acts of the penitent include contrition, confession,           1451,
and making amends. Contrition is sorrow for sin and                1455,
the resolution not to sin anymore. Confession to the               1459
priest is an essential element of the sacrament of penance.

All mortal sins of which penitents are conscious must             1456,
be confessed. Those who have committed a mortal sin               1457
should go to confession before receiving communion.
Everything possible must be done to make amends for
our sins.

Children should approach the sacrament of penance                 1457
before receiving Holy Communion for the first time.

The confessor is the servant of God's forgiveness, not            1466
its master. The minister should be joined to Christ's intention and love.

The doctrine and practice of indulgences are related to           1471
the sacrament of penance. An indulgence is the re-
mission of temporal punishment due to sins that have
been forgiven.

1480-83    Penance is a liturgical action. It can be celebrated in-
           dividually, communally, or in the case of urgent need,
           communally with general absolution.

## The Anointing of the Sick (n. 1499-1532)

1499       The church commends the sick to the suffering and
           glorified Lord through the sacrament of the anointing
           of the sick.

1503       Christ's compassion toward the sick and his many
           healings signify that God looks favorably on sick peo-
           ple and that the kingdom of God is at hand. The
           church has received this ministry from the Lord and
           strives to carry it out by the care it brings to the sick,
           bringing them the life-giving presence of Christ.

1508       The Holy Spirit gives certain people a special gift of
           healing, and thus reveals the power of the risen Christ.

1511       Among the seven sacraments, one is especially in-
           tended to comfort those who are ill: the anointing of
           the sick.

1513-15    The sacrament of the anointing of the sick is given to
           those who are seriously ill; that is, those in danger of
           death from sickness or old age. A sick person may be
           anointed before serious surgery.

1517       The anointing of the sick is a liturgical celebration and
           may take place at home, in the hospital, or the church.
           It may be celebrated for one sick person or for a group
           of people who are ill.

1520-21    The first grace of this sacrament is comfort, peace, and
           courage in the face of illness or the frailty of old age.
           The grace of this sacrament enables the sick to unite
           themselves more intimately with Christ's passion.

This sacrament is also given to those who are dying. It        1523
completes Christ's death and resurrection in us, just as
it began in baptism.

## Commentary

The Catechism links penance to Jesus' ministry of forgiveness
and his call for conversion. Conversion is viewed as an ongoing
process, which includes concern for the poor and the oppressed.
The text points out that sin is not merely a private matter, but
also an offense against the church. Therefore sin calls for a public
(sacramental) act that leads to reconciliation with the church.

The sacrament of penance has a complicated history with diverse forms and practices. In the early centuries public penance
prevailed. This was gradually replaced by private penance in
about the sixth century. This form originated with the Irish
monks, and although it was officially opposed for quite some
time, it eventually became the accepted, and then the required
norm. The "acts of the penitent" have varied, and some scholars
continue to maintain that the actual confession of sins is not integral to the sacrament. If this is true, the way could be opened
for a more liberal use of general absolution.

The term "mortal sin" is used in the Catechism. Since "mortal" implies a state of death, many theologians prefer to use
terms like "serious" or "grave sin" for individual evil actions.
The term "fundamental option," although it is not used in the
Catechism, has gained acceptance among many moral theologians and religious educators as a way of describing the direction of one's moral life. It provides a context in which to situate
individual moral choices.

The issue of first penance before communion for childen remains a point of controversy among religious educators, parents,
and pastoral leaders. Here the distinction between useful and
necessary is helpful. If celebrated properly, first penance at such
an early age can be useful. Canonically, penance is only necessary for those in serious sin. There seems to be a consensus
that young children do not have sufficient moral awareness or
responsibility to commit serious sins, and thus are not obliged to
confess their sins before receiving communion. Parents and re-

ligious educators who know the children are in the best position to decide the appropriate time for first penance.

Belief in the temporal punishment due to sin and the practice of indulgences are often not part of the "sense of the faithful" or the pastoral practice of the contemporary church. Some wonder if the teaching about the temporal punishment due to sin doesn't also place limits on God's gracious forgiveness. Others see indulgences as an obstacle to ecumenical dialogue.

The new forms of celebrating the sacrament of penance (face-to-face confession and communal services with individual confession) have not gained a broad acceptance, at least in the United States. As a result, many hope that general absolution will someday be celebrated more liberally.

The sacrament of the anointing of the sick is appropriately linked to Jesus' ministry to the sick and handicapped. It is also linked to his passion and the redemptive power of suffering. Historically, this sacrament for the sick could be celebrated by family members who would bring the blessed oil home with them from church. In the eighth century the emphasis shifted from all sick people to just those who were dying, and only priests were allowed to administer the sacrament. From that era until recent times the sacrament was known as Extreme Unction (Last Anointing) and was used only just before death.

Today, pastoral practice takes a broad view of "serious sickness," and the sacrament of the anointing is administered liberally. Unfortunately, the shortage of clergy has placed limits on the availability of this sacrament. In response, some people want the church to consider expanding the administration of this sacrament beyond the ordained priesthood.

The healing ministry both inside and outside the context of this sacrament has broadened in recent decades, especially through the efforts of the charismatic movement. They have shown the church that healing can touch physical, emotional, and psychological aspects of the person's being.

Liberation theology has demonstrated new facets of this sacrament, especially in times of violence and oppression. It is in the healing ministry that ministers have found themselves in close solidarity with the oppressed.

The Catechism also stresses the ecclesial dimension of this sacrament. In the celebration of this sacrament, the church prays for the sick at the same time it is nurtured by the redemptive power of the suffering of the faithful. Communal celebrations of healing have in some areas become quite popular, and effectively emphasize the ecclesial dimension of the anointing of the sick.

### Suggested Readings

Brennan, Patrick. *Penance and Reconciliation.* Chicago: Thomas More Press, 1986.

Dallen, James. *The Reconciling Community: The Rite of Penance.* Collegeville, MN: Liturgical Press, 1991.

Empereur, James L. *Prophetic Anointing.* Collegeville, MN: Liturgical Press (Glazier Books), 1982.

Gusmer, Charles. *And You Visited Me: Sacramental Ministry to the Sick and Dying.* Collegeville, MN: Liturgical Press (Pueblo Books), 1984.

Osborne, Kenan B. *Reconciliation and Justification: The Sacrament and Its Theology.* Mahwah, NJ: Paulist Press. 1990.

Rahner, Karl. *Penance in the Early Church.* New York: Crossroad, 1982.

# Chapter Three:
# The Sacraments in Service of Communion
### (n. 1533-1699)

### Summary

This chapter treats holy orders and matrimony, sacraments that contribute to both personal salvation and the service of others. The ordained priesthood has its roots in Israel, the priestly kingdom, and God's chosen people. This priesthood is fulfilled in Christ. The ministerial priesthood represents Christ and the church.

There are three levels in the sacrament of holy orders: bishop, priest, and deacon. Ordination is conferred by a bishop laying on hands and saying a specific prayer. Only a baptized man can be ordained. This sacrament confers an indelible character and a unique grace of the Spirit.

Marriage was established by God from the beginning of creation. In his preaching Jesus teaches the original meaning of marriage. In the Latin (Roman rite) church the spouses are the ministers of marriage. Marital consent must be free and should be celebrated in a public liturgy. The sacrament of matrimony effects a permanent bond and conveys the special grace of the sacrament. Married love requires unity, indissolubility, and fidelity. It must be open to new life. The family has been called the "domestic church." Jesus also teaches that virginity can be lived for the sake of the kingdom. Those leading the single life are close to the Lord's heart and deserve the concern of the church.

### Orders (n. 1533-1600)

1545     Christ is the one true priest, all others are his ministers. Christ's one priesthood is made present through the ministerial priesthood.

1546     The entire community of believers is priestly. The faithful exercise their baptismal priesthood through their participation in Christ's mission.

1547     The ministerial priesthood is at the service of the common priesthood. It assists all Christians' baptismal grace and is a means which Christ uses to build up and direct the church.

1551     The sacrament of holy orders communicates a sacred power, which is Christ's power. The use of this power must be modeled after Christ, who by love became the servant of all.

1552     The task of the ministerial priesthood is to represent Christ as head of the church. Priests also act on behalf of the faithful in the name of the whole church, especially when they offer the eucharist.

Episcopal consecration confers the fullness of the sacra-      1557-58
ment of orders. This consecration confers the offices of
teaching, governing, and sanctifying.

As Christ's vicar, each bishop is entrusted with the             1560
pastoral care of a particular church (diocese). He also
shares collegially with other bishops in their concern
for the universal church.

Priests are delegated by bishops to collaborate in a sub-       1562
ordinate capacity in carrying out the apostolic mission
entrusted to them by Christ.

Priests are consecrated by the sacrament of holy orders      1564-66
to preach the gospel, shepherd the faithful, and celebrate divine worship in the image of Christ. They exercise their sacred ministry especially in eucharistic
worship.

Deacons assist the bishop and priests in the celebration        1570
of the liturgy, especially in the celebration of the eucharist. They distribute communion, witness to and
bless marriages, preach the gospel, preside at funerals,
and carry out the ministries of charity.

Only a baptized man can validly receive sacred ordina-          1577
tion. Jesus chose men to form the college of the twelve
apostles, and the apostles did the same when they
chose co-workers to succeed them. The college of bishops, with whom priests are united, makes the college
of the twelve an ever-present reality. The church considers itself bound by this choice of the Lord, and for
this reason the ordination of women is not possible.

The ordained ministers of the Latin (Roman rite)               1580
church, with the exception of permanent deacons, are
normally chosen from among celibates. In the Eastern
churches married men can be ordained to the diaconate and priesthood, but not to the episcopacy.

*Marriage* (n. 1601-1666)

1601        In the marriage covenant a man and a woman establish a partnership for their entire lives. This covenant is ordered to the well being of the partners and the procreation and upbringing of children. Christ has raised this covenant to the dignity of a sacrament for baptized persons.

1603-04     The Creator established the marriage covenant as an intimate partnership of life and love. God created man and woman through love, and in turn calls them to love, the innate vocation of every human person. God is love and created man and woman in that image. Their mutual love expresses their likeness to God.

1605        Man and woman were created for one another. Woman is man's equal partner, living in complete intimacy with him. Given to man by God as a helper, she thus represents God, from whom comes all help.

1613,       The church attaches great importance to the presence
1623        of Jesus at the wedding feast at Cana. His presence was a confirmation of the goodness of marriage. It proclaims that from that time forward, marriage is an effective sign of Christ's presence. In the Latin (Roman rite) church the spouses are the ministers of the sacrament of marriage and confer the sacrament of marriage on each other.

1628,       The consent to marry must be a free act of the will ex-
1632        pressed by both persons getting married, without coercion or serious fear. The marriage is invalid if such freedom is lacking. Preparation for marriage is extremely important, so that the consent of the spouses might be free and responsible.

1640        God established the marriage bond in such a way that a marriage between baptized persons can never be dissolved if there is free consent and the marriage has been consummated.

The grace of this sacrament perfects the couple's love, strengthens their indissoluble unity, and helps them in their own holiness. It also assists them in the upbringing of their children.                    1641

Marriage aims at a deeply personal unity, a communion of one heart and soul. Marriage demands indissolubility, fidelity, mutual self-giving, and openness to children.                    1643

The equal personal dignity of woman and man must be recognized in the couple's mutual and total love.                    1645

Married love requires by its very nature the spouses' inviolable fidelity. They give themselves to each other definitively.                    1646

Believing families are centers of living, radiant faith. The family is a "domestic church," a community of grace and prayer, and a school of Christian love.                    1656-57

Single persons are especially close to Jesus' heart and deserve the affection and attentive concern of the church and of their pastors.                    1658

### Sacramentals (n. 1667-1699)

Sacramentals are sacred signs that dispose people to receive the chief effect of a sacrament, and make holy various occasions of life.                    1667

A sacramental does not confer grace, but prepares people to receive grace and disposes them to cooperate with it.                    1670

1674,
1679   The religious sense of Christians finds expression in various forms of piety surrounding the church's sacramental life. The church fosters forms of popular devotion that express the gospel and enrich Christian life.

## Commentary

The Catechism links the ordained priesthood to Christ, the one priest. The priesthood of all believers is mentioned again, and the ordained priesthood is viewed as being at its service. This marks a decided move from the traditional notion of priesthood, which was essentially liturgical and not adequately linked with Christ.

The priesthood began as a ministry of service, but evolved into a liturgical office, with emphasis on "powers" rather than service. The Catechism reclaims an earlier perspective of priesthood and shifts the emphasis of priesthood to preaching, teaching, and pastoral service.

Many priests and faithful prefer this broader and more pastoral notion of priesthood. Therefore there is often apprehension that today's shortage of priests will lead us to place priests in charge of clusters of parishes. This could make the priests' sacramental role once again predominant, and perhaps diminish their pastoral contact with the people.

In the future, the challenge will be to see how the ordained priesthood can be more closely related to and in partnership with the common priesthood of the faithful. Catholics should be made more aware of sharing in the priesthood of Christ by virtue of their baptism, and of their responsibilities for ministry. An equality of the sexes in this area will be a struggle for some time to come.

The Second Vatican Council clarified the role of the bishop and the meaning of episcopal ordination, clearly emphasizing the collegial authority of bishops. Subsequent to the Council, theologians called for a clarification of the meaning of the ordained priesthood. When the bishop is described as having the fullness of the priesthood, and the ordained priest is viewed as a subordinate delegate, the priest loses uniqueness and autonomy. In addition, the scandals of a few have marred the image of the many. There is a need to bring to light the extraordinary pastoral service and exemplary lives of the majority of Catholic priests today.

The diaconate was restored to the church after Vatican II, and found an enthusiastic response in the United States and some other countries. The Catechism underscores the liturgical responsibilities of the deacon. More emphasis needs to be made on the pastoral and administrative possibilities for the diaconate. Since many wives of deacons have shared in their formation, the question often arises as to whether they might also share in this ministry. Some church historians have pointed out a historical precedence for the office of deaconess. Would this not suggest the possibility of calling women to such ordination?

The arguments against the ordination of women seem to have narrowed down to one: the choice by Jesus of men to be the twelve apostles, and the belief that the college of bishops and priests carry on this apostolic role.

Biblical and historical studies raise many questions in this area, however, and there is still much to be studied and considered. First of all, it is extremely difficult to locate Jesus' explicit intentions regarding the forms of ministry or priesthood to be exercised in the community. He did not leave behind an established church order. Rather, Jesus promised to send the Spirit to his followers, and under the guidance of the Spirit, ministerial forms developed gradually within the church as needs arose.

As we noted earlier, the Twelve seems to symbolize the heads of the twelve tribes of Israel, and looks forward to the establishment of the New Israel. As for the term "apostle," little is known of the ministry of Jesus' original apostles, other than that of Peter. Moreover, as the apostles died, there was apparently no move to replace them. The notion of apostle also seems to have, at times, a broader connotation than the Twelve. Paul speaks of himself as an apostle and refers to other church leaders as apostles.

As for apostolic succession, this notion seems to have come into prominence in the third and fourth centuries. Its purpose does not seem to be to exclusively indicate a traceable line of ministers, but to authentically link the church's current teaching with the teaching that Jesus gave to his original apostles.

77

Historical and biblical studies reveal a diversity of ministerial forms in the early church. Ministers were called forth according to their gifts, irrespective of gender, marital status, or ethnic background. Ordination to priesthood seems to appear first in the second century, and eventually a hierarchical and clerical model of priestly ministry evolved. Cultural and political influences contributed to the development of ministry, and each age has had its own forms. It seems likely that the contemporary era will gradually develop the forms of ministry that are both needed and appropriate for the people and the times.

Celibacy does not seem essential to the priesthood. It has been a legal norm in the Latin (Roman rite) church since the twelfth century. Many political, cultural, and theological factors were at work in its appearance and gradual implementation. Dramatic declines in priestly vocations in North America and Europe have raised questions about changing this legislation in the future. The practice of accepting former Episcopal priests, who are married, into the Catholic priesthood has caused further confusion about this norm.

The Catechism reflects the shifts that have gone on in Catholic teaching with regard to the sacrament of matrimony. The emphasis shifts from contract and procreation to an understanding of marriage that focuses on love, covenant, partnership, and the well-being of the partners. It is in this context that the family grows and is nurtured. It is also within this framework that the sacred promises of fidelity and permanency are made. More attention to sexuality and its importance in marriage might be given in catechesis than is found in the text.

The Catechism emphasizes the equality of the sexes and the need for partnership and intimacy, but then uses the word "helper" in reference to the wife. Greater recognition needs to be given to the many changing patterns and shifting roles that are taking place in contemporary marriages.

The need for marriage preparation is mentioned in the Catechism. Considerable research on the sociological, psychological, and theological dimensions of marriage is now available, but couples preparing for marriage are often not adequately familiarized with this information. Preparation is often perfunctory at best. This is an area of pastoral care where investment in personnel and finances is sorely needed. In addition, resources are needed to provide counseling and assistance to married couples.

Given the dynamic notion of sacrament found in the earlier part of this section, reference to the sacrament of matrimony being accomplished by consent and consummation seems inappropriate. Many theologians maintain that the marriage bond evolves over time, and cannot be limited to such legal and physical considerations. Moreover, some question whether many of the baptized actually have the faith necessary to celebrate marriage as a sacrament.

Vatican II promoted the notion of the family being the "domestic church." One would hope that the church moves from rhetoric to reality in this regard. In order for this to happen, serious consideration has to be given to both the family's capacity to worship in the home and the married couple's ability to participate fully in the ministries of the church.

The Catechism could have devoted more time and attention to the single life. It needs to be stressed that the single life is a calling in its own right. More recognition also might have been given to the fact that a considerable proportion of Catholics are single: those who never married, the separated or divorced, single parents, and those who have been widowed. A clear and significant place in the community of the faithful needs to be defined for these members of the community.

More attention in the future might be given to enriching the sacramental theology of marriage. Other areas not covered in the Catechism but in need of further consideration include the role of romantic love in marriage; the sacredness of marriage in other churches, religions, and even outside of religion; the family as a unit of resistance in areas where there is political oppression; and alternatives to the annulment process.

# Suggested Readings

## Order and Ministry

Bernier, Paul. *Ministry in the Church: A Historical and Pastoral Approach.* Mystic, CT: Twenty-Third Publications, 1992.

Dolan, Jay, et al. *Transforming Parish Ministry: The Changing Roles of Catholic Clergy, Laity and Women Religious.* New York: Crossroad, 1990.

Goergen, Donald, ed. *Being a Priest Today.* Collegeville, MN: Liturgical Press, 1992.

Osborne, Kenan B. *Priesthood: A History of Ordained Ministry in the Roman Catholic Church.* Mahwah, NJ: Paulist Press, 1988.

_____. *Ministry: Lay Ministry in the Catholic Church.* Mahwah, NJ: Paulist Press, 1993.

O'Grady, John. *Disciples and Leaders.* Mahwah, NJ: Paulist Press, 1991.

Rausch, Thomas. *Priesthood Today.* Mahwah, NJ: Paulist Press, 1992.

Schillebeeckx, Edward. *The Church with a Human Face: A New Expanded Theology of Ministry.* New York: Crossroad, 1985.


## Marriage

Dominian, Jack. *Dynamics of Marriage.* Mystic, CT: Twenty-Third Publications, 1993.

Hart, Thomas, and Kathleen Fischer. *Promises to Keep.* Mahwah, NJ: Paulist Press, 1991.

Lawler, Michael. *Marriage and Sacrament: A Theology of Christian Marriage.* Collegeville, MN: Liturgical Press, 1993.

Mackin, Theodore. *The Marital Sacrament.* Mahwah, NJ: Paulist Press, 1989.

Roberts, Challon O'Hearn, and William P. Roberts. *Partners in Intimacy: Living Christian Marriage Today.* Mahwah, NJ: Paulist Press, 1988.

Martin, Thomas, M. *The Challenge of Christian Marriage.* Mahwah, NJ: Paulist Press, 1990.

# PART THREE

# LIFE IN CHRIST

# Part Three:
# Life in Christ

## Summary

Part Three deals with Christian living and morality. It comes after the Catechism's discussion of the creed (Part One) and the sacraments (Part Two) because the Christian life is the attempt to live out the faith with the assistance of the grace that comes through the sacraments. Section One of Part Three discusses the nature of being human and the gift of salvation that brings human nature to its fulfillment and ultimate happiness. Section Two explains in great detail how the Ten Commandments can be viewed as the basis of morality.

# Section One:
# Our Human Vocation:
# Life in the Spirit

## Chapter One:
## The Dignity of the Human Person
### (n. 1700-1876)

### Summary
The dignity of the human person is the key theme of Chapter One. Human dignity is rooted in the fact that every human being is created in the image of God. Each person is called to share in the divine life and thus to enjoy ultimate happiness. Inalienable human rights, such as the right to shape one's life according to responsible and free choices and the right to receive fair and equal treatment from others, flow from this fact. Respect for human dignity means that people must never be forced to act against their consciences nor kept from acting in accord with their consciences. An individual's conscience, however, must be properly formed. Sin is an act, word, or desire contrary to the judgment of a rightly formed conscience.

*The human person (n. 1700-1876)*

Human dignity is rooted in the fact that every human being is created in God's image.

1700-02, 1704

1718     God has planted a natural desire for happiness in each human being, which directs people toward God.

1720,    Ultimate happiness, which is a free gift from God, is to
1722     be attained through the coming of God's kingdom.

1723     Christian morality rests upon this call to ultimate happiness.

1731-32  Human dignity includes the freedom to shape one's life according to the choices a person makes. Insofar as a person freely performs an action, it can be praised or criticized.

1735     Responsibility for individual actions can be lessened or suppressed by the use of force against the agent, or by ignorance, fear, and other psychological or social factors.

1733,    When people deviate from the moral law, they violate
1742     the most authentic sense of freedom, that is, the capacity freely to collaborate in God's work within the church and the world.

1750     Three factors determine the morality of an action: the act itself, the person's intention, and the circumstances.

1753     A good intention does not justify an evil action; an evil intention corrupts an otherwise good action.

1754,    Circumstances can increase or diminish the moral
1756     quality of actions and a person's responsibility for performing them. Circumstances cannot, however, make an evil act good.

1767     "Passions," which usually accompany actions, are neither good nor evil. They become morally good or evil to the extent that they assist or hinder a person's perception of the good and the will to do the good.

Conscience is the capacity of every human person to perceive the moral quality of a specific act which he or she intends to do, is in the process of doing, or has already done.

1778

People must never be forced to act against their conscience nor kept from acting in accord with their conscience.

1782, 1790

A person's conscience, however, must be informed by God's word and by reason. The formation of conscience is a lifelong task and process.

1783-85

Virtue, which is a firm and habitual disposition to do what is good, can guide one's feelings and conduct in accordance with faith and reason.

1803-04

The central moral virtues are prudence, justice, fortitude (courage), and temperance (self-control). These virtues can be acquired through education and perseverance in doing good actions. They find support in the theological virtues of faith, hope, and love, which are gifts from God.

1805, 1810, 1812-13

Love is the theological virtue by which people love God above all things and love their neighbor as themselves for the love of God.

1822

Christian love raises the natural human ability to love to a new level, so that people begin to love as God loves. Love unites the other virtues and inspires people to live out all the other virtues.

1827

Sin is any act, word, or desire contrary to the judgment of a rightly informed conscience. Sin wounds human nature and harms a person's relationship with God and with others.

1849-50

1854-55    Some sins are more serious than others. Knowingly and deliberately to commit a serious infraction of God's law is a mortal sin. It kills in the human heart the love by which people love God above all things and love their neighbors as themselves.

1862-63    Venial sin is a less serious infraction. Although it does not destroy a person's relationship with God, it weakens love in the human heart.

1865       Repeated sinful actions can cause or reinforce a pattern of sinful behavior, but they cannot entirely destroy the moral sense embedded in each human person.

1868       People share responsibility for the sins of others when they participate in those actions, praise them, refuse to reveal the sinfulness of the action, or do not try to stop the person from sinning.

1869       Sinful structures or institutions that encourage people to sin are called "social sins."

## Commentary

Part Three of the Catechism initially describes the Christian life as life in the Holy Spirit. As a consequence of justification and sanctification, Christians have become temples of the Holy Spirit. This means that God's Spirit has renewed them inwardly not only so that they can see clearly what is good and what is evil, but also so that their actions will be guided by the divine Spirit. In the development of this theme, Part Three emphasizes obedience to the "objective" moral law as the primary way to live in the Spirit.

Contemporary theology offers some insights that complement the Catechism's explanation of the Christian moral life. For example, the gift of life in the Spirit, instead of being interpreted as a gift given primarily to facilitate obedience to specific moral laws, can be understood as a gift given primarily to enable people to discern how the values embodied in the life, death, and resurrection of Jesus can be lived out in diverse situations. Such an interpretation is attentive to the difference between enduring moral values or changeless principles, on the one hand, and the historically conditioned norms or applications that express them, on the other. It is also cognizant of the fact that moral decision making is often more complex than simply finding and applying a specific rule to a particular situation. Because they are keenly aware of the complexity of moral decision making, many contemporary moral theologians emphasize the need for discernment and proportionate reasoning rather than speaking exclusively of law and obedience.

One of the current central metaphors for understanding the Christian moral life is the metaphor of responsibility. When responsibility is made a central metaphor, the Christian moral life becomes a life of response to the call of God and the needs of one's neighbors. Relationship to and with others, not sheer obedience to specific moral laws, takes on decisive significance. From this perspective, the question "What ought I to do?" needs to be complemented by the question "What ought I to be?" Whereas the first question focuses on the action to be done or avoided, the second question focuses on the agent who is considering the action.

Attempting to balance the orientation of much pre-Vatican II moral theology with its emphasis on the inherent goodness or evil of specific actions, some theologians today emphasize the attitudes and dispositions of the moral agent. They define the principal moral question as "What is God enabling me to be and requiring me to do in this situation?"

Using a relational approach to moral theology and moral decision making provides a helpful frame of reference for considering the issue of sin. If sin and virtue are seen as indicators of the quality of an individual's relationship with God and others, mortal sin can be defined as a fundamental breaking off of one's relationship with God and others. This raises the question of whether a fundamental turning away from God can be accomplished in one sinful act. By emphasizing the notion of responsibility and relationship, one can move beyond the

Catechism's basic recognition of the deleterious effects of sin upon one's relationship with God and others to a fuller understanding of the issues of conscience and sin.

## Suggested Readings

Crossin, John W. *What Are They Saying About Virtue?* Mahwah, NJ: Paulist Press, 1985.

Dwyer, John C. *Foundations of Christian Ethics*. Mahwah, NJ: Paulist Press, 1987.

Gula, Richard M. *What Are They Saying About Moral Norms?* Mahwah, NJ: Paulist Press, 1982.

_____. *Reason Informed by Faith*. Mahwah, NJ: Paulist Press, 1989.

John Paul II, Pope. *The Splendor of Truth*. Encyclical Letter. Washington, DC: United States Catholic Conference, 1993.

O'Connell, Timothy E. *Principles for a Catholic Morality*. Revised Edition. San Francisco: HarperSanFrancisco, 1990.

# Chapter Two:
# The Human Community
### (n. 1877-1948)

## Summary

Human beings are social and naturally form various types of communities. Christians believe that people are called to establish among themselves a community based on equality, respect, and love. This type of community finds its model in the union that exists among the persons of the trinity. It is the nature of the human community (society) to work for the common good of all its members. Respect for the dignity of the human person is the foundation of social justice, and social justice is an integral part of the common good.

*The human community (n. 1877-1948)*

1878-79    To live in society is a requirement of human nature. To
           establish among people the kind of union that is re-

alized among the persons of the trinity is the task of
human society.

Society is called to promote spiritual values and sup-     1886
port the exercise of virtue.

The inner conversion of the hearts of individuals is an     1888
ongoing task. It is the first step in the transformation of
unjust social structures.

In a just society, legitimate authority works for the     1897-98,
common good of all the members through morally ac-          1903
ceptable means.

The common good presupposes respect for each per-     1907
son. This begins with respect for the proper freedom of
every individual.

The common good requires the social well-being and     1908
development of the group. This means that authorities
in society must make available to each member of society those things needed to lead a truly human life:
food, clothing, healthcare, work, education, culture,
the right to establish a family, and so on.

Every person should promote the common good and     1913-16
support those institutions that improve the condition
of human life.

Because the entire human race constitutes the one hu-     1911
man family of God, there should exist some international organization dedicated to promoting the
universal common good.

Social justice is an integral part of the common good     1928
which society must promote and protect.

The foundation of social justice is respect for the dig-     1929-30

89

nity of the human person and the rights that flow from this dignity.

1933-35    All people, including those who think or act differently and those who are perceived to be enemies, enjoy equal dignity. Consequently, every kind of discrimination that affects a person's fundamental rights is to be rejected as contrary to God's will.

1931       To respect the dignity of another person is to regard the other person as another self, who is entitled to live in a manner worthy of human beings.

1937       Differences among people are part of the divine plan. God wills that people should need one another.

1939-41    International solidarity is a requirement of the Christian life. It involves effort on behalf of a more just social order and an equitable distribution of material and spiritual goods.

## Commentary

This chapter builds upon the previous chapter by making respect for the dignity of each and every individual the basis of authentic human community. The Catechism explains how concern for the common good must be the obligation of both rulers and citizens in any community. It is in this discussion of the common good that the theme of social justice is introduced.

The church has made the theme of social justice a central category in contemporary theological reflection and witness. It stands to reason that this theme is quite evident in the Catechism. One might wish, however, that it was developed further. The Catechism speaks of unjust social structures, economic and social inequalities among nations, and the principle of human solidarity. Unfortunately the term "preferential option for the poor," which figures prominently in other recent church documents, is not mentioned in this section on social justice. Moreover, the Catechism does not fully explicate the connection between social justice and religious faith.

Contemporary theology, especially liberation theology in its many forms, has developed this connection in greater detail. It emphasizes the point that people cannot claim to have religious faith in a God of love and justice unless they also address the social evils in the world. From this perspective, one cannot authentically love God without loving and creating justice for all one's neighbors in the human family. In addition, liberation theology suggests that the human person must be viewed as an inseparable union of body and spirit, and that salvation must address both the material and spiritual needs of the human person. This emphasis complements the Catechism's focus on the primacy of spiritual needs. In a similar fashion, contemporary liberation theology augments the Catechism's focus on individuals and their inner conversion by bringing attention to the dynamics of social class and the need for structural change as a means to greater social justice.

## Suggested Readings

Boff, Leonardo, and Clodovis Boff. *Introducing Liberation Theology.* Maryknoll, NY: Orbis Books, 1988.

Coleman, John A., ed. *One Hundred Years of Catholic Social Thought.* Maryknoll, NY: Orbis Books, 1991.

Dorr, Donal. *Option for the Poor: 100 Years of Catholic Social Thought.* Revised edition. Maryknoll, NY: Orbis Books, 1992.

Gremillion, Joseph, ed. *The Gospel of Peace and Justice.* Maryknoll, NY: Orbis Books, 1976.

Hollenbach, David. *Justice, Peace, and Human Rights: American Catholic Social Ethics in a Pluralistic World.* New York: Crossroad, 1989.

Walsh, Michael, and Brian Davies, eds. *Proclaiming Justice and Peace: Papal Documents from Rerum Novarum to Centesimus Annus.* Mystic, CT: Twenty-Third Publications, 1991.

# Chapter Three:
# God's Gift of Salvation:
# Law and Grace
## (n. 1949-2051)

### Summary
People are called individually to experience ultimate happiness with God and collectively to form just and loving human communities. Because they are wounded by sin, people need divine assistance to attain these goals. There are two principal ways in which God helps human beings to reach these goals: through revelation of the moral law, which guides human behavior, and through the gift of grace, which enables people to live according to the moral law.

*Law and Grace (n. 1949-2051)*

1949    Called to happiness but wounded by sin, the human race needs God's gift of salvation. God's help comes through Christ, and by means of the moral law that guides all people and the grace that sustains them.

1950    The moral law, which derives from God's wisdom, prescribes the rules of conduct leading to the happiness promised by God.

1953    The moral law finds its fullness in Christ, who is the way of perfection.

1954    Natural law expresses the original moral sense, engraved in the soul of every human being, by which people can rationally know what is good and what is evil.

1956-58    Although applications of the natural law vary greatly and should be adapted to the diversity of life's conditions, the general precepts of the natural law are universal and permanent.

Because not everyone clearly and immediately perceives the precepts of the natural law, it has been necessary for God to reveal the moral law.      1960

The law of Moses, summed up in the Ten Commandments, is the first stage of the revealed law.      1961-62

The law of the Gospel, summed up in the Sermon on the Mount and the Golden Rule, is the perfection of both the natural and the revealed law.      1965, 1970

The law of the Gospel does not add precepts to the law of Moses, but calls for a reform of the heart which stands at the root of all human actions.      1968

The grace of the Holy Spirit justifies people. It brings about inner conversion, cleanses them from their sins, and begins a spiritual renewal.      1987, 1989

By uniting people through faith and love to Christ's passion and resurrection, the Spirit makes them sharers in the divine life.      1988

The grace by which people participate in the divine life, as well as their preparation to accept this grace, is a free and unmerited gift from God.      1997-98, 2001

Grace calls people to cooperate freely with God's initiative in their lives.      1993, 2002

The spiritual progress made in love brings people into an ever more intimate union with Christ, and through Christ with the trinity.      2014

Christians receive from the church the teachings of      2030

Christ's law and the grace of the sacraments to sustain them on their spiritual journey.

2033,    The teaching authority of the church's pastors in moral
2038     matters is exercised ordinarily in catechesis and preaching, with the help of theologians and spiritual authors.

2035     The charism of infallibility extends to those things which have been divinely revealed and to those elements of doctrine or morality without which the saving, revealed truths of faith cannot be explained or observed.

2039     Ultimately there can be no opposition or contradiction between individual conscience and the natural or revealed moral law.

2031,    The moral life is united to and nourished by the li-
2041     turgical life.

## Commentary

The Catechism states that Christians are called to a life of obedience and holiness. In this, they are to emulate the perfection of their heavenly Father. The Catechism explains that moral perfection comes by following the path of individual self-denial and spiritual struggle. It does not, however, over-emphasize eternal rewards and punishments as the consequences of a moral life. In fact, the section on merit is quite brief and stresses the fact that human merits are ultimately gifts from God. Although the Catechism's reserve in speaking about punishment, reward, and merit can help to check the temptation to reduce "doing the right thing" to a utilitarian way of insuring one's own salvation, the discussion of the moral law can be enriched by additional considerations.

Some moral theologians point out, for example, that the call to emulate God's perfection can be rightly interpreted to mean a call to imitate God's extravagant beneficence. This is best expressed by loving others without distinction. From this perspective, imitating God's love means becoming a disciple of Jesus in service to others more than it means attaining individual virtue for its own sake. When imitation of God's command is viewed in this way, personal holiness is understood to be the consequence of being faithful in one's actions to Jesus' call to minister to others in the world, rather than the consequence of withdrawing from others and the world in order to practice the virtue of self-denial. In a similar way, perfection is then understood to result not from an exclusive focus upon personal self-improvement, but from compassionate attention to the needs of all others. (See Matthew 5:43–48 on being made perfect as the heavenly Father is perfect.)

The Catechism further develops the idea that obedience to the moral law leads to the happiness and salvation promised by God. Some theologians expand this understanding of the moral life to include a greater role for personal discernment of one's moral responsibility to God and neighbor. They appeal to the image of Jesus in the gospels, a Jesus who challenged those around him to take responsibility for their response to his proclamation of the in-breaking kingdom of God. They note that the historical Jesus used parables regularly to challenge prevalent attitudes and behaviors in his religion and culture. They remind people that Jesus not only reinterpreted, but also sometimes sharply challenged, the moral law of his day.

Other theologians draw upon the resources of psychology to understand the stages of moral development. Drawing upon this information, they conclude that the relational-responsible model of Christian morality is in tune with a more mature stage of moral development. They understand that the mature individual has gone beyond an unreflective conformity to conventional laws to a personal, conscientious responsibility for moral decision making.

Still other theologians enrich the understanding of moral law by distinguishing between the kinds of norms in which the law is expressed. These theologians draw attention to an important distinction between formal norms, which deal with essential human attitudes, and material norms, which deal with specific human actions. Building upon this distinction, one might suggest, for example, that a formal norm (such as: respect life) allows no exceptions, whereas a material norm (such as: do not kill) might allow exceptions. From this perspective the formal norm (respect life) provides an exceptionless guide to the kind of person we ought to be and the kind of attitudes we ought to hold. It does not, however, describe specifically how we are to respect life. That requires a process of conscientious discernment. In a similar way, the material norm (do not kill) can be understood to present a generally applicable guide to action, which nonetheless allows exceptions (for example: killing an unjust aggressor in order to protect one's own life).

Making important, yet sometimes seemingly fine distinctions such as these can be helpful in understanding other aspects of the Christian moral life. For example, when the Catechism speaks of the natural law, it affirms, on the one hand, that the most basic precepts of the natural law are universal and permanent. Yet it admits, on the other hand, that the natural law needs to be adapted to fit the diversity of places, times, and circumstances. Contemporary theology has devoted considerable reflection to questions about which aspects of natural law are immutable and which aspects are historically conditioned and therefore open to change. Because the Catechism does not fully explain what it means when it says that the rules of natural law are *substantially* valid and because it does not elaborate on *how* applications of the natural law vary greatly while its principles remain universal, readers will need to pay attention to the contemporary discussion of these issues.

## Suggested Readings

Curran, Charles E., and Richard A. McCormick, eds. *Readings in Moral Theology, No. 2: The Distinctiveness of Christian Ethics.* Mahwah, NJ: Paulist Press, 1980.

Overberg, Kenneth R. *Conscience in Conflict: How to Make Moral Choices.* Cincinnati: St. Anthony Messenger Press, 1991.

Sloyan, Gerard S. *Catholic Morality Revisited: Origins and Contemporary Challenges.* Mystic, CT: Twenty-Third Publications, 1990.

# Section Two:
# The Ten Commandments

### Summary

Section Two of Part Three presents the Ten Commandments as the basis of Christian morality. In this section, the decalogue is viewed as a privileged expression of the natural law which is engraved in the human heart. The text emphasizes that love of God and love of neighbor are intimately bound together. Chapter One discusses the moral obligation to love God and to offer God regular and authentic worship, as expressed in the first three commandments. The fourth through tenth commandments, which address proper conduct toward one's neighbor, are the subject of Chapter Two.

*The Ten Commandments (n. 2052-2082)*

To be a disciple of Christ involves obeying the Ten Commandments, whose full significance and spirit has been revealed by Jesus.   2053-54, 2056

The decalogue must be interpreted in light of the two-fold commandment to love God with our entire heart, soul, and mind, and to love our neighbor as ourselves.   2055

2060-62   The Ten Commandments were revealed by God as part of the divine covenant with God's people. They spell out the implications of belonging to this covenant.

2069      Because the decalogue forms an integrated whole, people cannot love their neighbor without blessing God and they cannot worship God without loving their neighbor.

2070-71   The decalogue contains a privileged expression of the natural law, which can be known through reason as well as through revelation.

2072      It is a Christian's moral duty to keep the serious obligations contained in the Ten Commandments.

# Chapter One:
# You Shall Love the Lord Your God
### (n. 2083-2195)

*The First Commandment: I am the Lord your God. You shall have no other gods before me. (n. 2083-2141)*

2086,     The first commandment summons people to place
2090,     complete faith and trust in God, to hope that God will
2093      enable them to keep the commandments of love, and to love God above all things.

2095-96,  Religion can dispose people to love God; the first act of
2105      religion is worship. To worship God is to recognize God as creator, savior, lord of everything that exists, and source of infinite and merciful love. All people are obliged to worship God authentically.

Christians have the social duty of awakening in each person the love of the true and the good. They must fulfill this duty without forcing anyone to act against his or her convictions in religious matters. 2105-06

The right to religious liberty is a natural and civil right that must be respected by political authorities. 2108

The first commandment forbids people to honor anything as a god—for example, power, money, pleasure—other than the one true God. Consequently, this commandment repudiates idolatry, superstition, and all forms of divination, magic, or sorcery. 2110, 2112-13, 2116-17

Sacrilege (profaning sacred things), simony (buying or selling spiritual powers), and putting God to the test are sins against the first commandment. 2118

Inasmuch as it rejects or denies the existence of God, atheism is a sin against the first commandment. Believers, however, often contribute to the spread of atheism around them by giving offense in their religious and moral lives, falsely explaining religious doctrines, or concealing the true features of God. 2125

The veneration of sacred images is not a violation of the first commandment insofar as the person represented by the image is venerated rather than the image itself. Veneration is not the same as adoration, which is owed to God alone. 2132

*The Second Commandment: You shall not make wrongful use of the name of the Lord your God. (n. 2142-2167)*

The second commandment reminds people that God's name is holy and that they must not abuse it. 2143

Blasphemy is a violation of this commandment. It con- 2148

sists in uttering against God words of hatred or reproach, using God's name as a cover for criminal practices, or failing to respect God. The prohibition against blasphemy extends to words against the church, the saints, and sacred objects.

2150,
2152     To take a false oath or to commit perjury is a violation of the second commandment.

2154     When sworn oaths are made for serious and just reasons (e.g., in court), swearing an oath is not a violation of this commandment.

*The Third Commandment: Remember to keep holy the sabbath day. (n. 2168-2195)*

2168-69,
2172     The sabbath, which recalls the completion of the first creation, is a model for humanity: If God rested and was refreshed on the seventh day, people also ought to refrain from everyday work and be refreshed.

2174-75     Christians celebrate Sunday rather than the Jewish sabbath because Christ's resurrection occurred on Sunday and signifies a new creation.

2176     To celebrate the Lord's day on Sunday fulfills the moral obligation to offer God visible, public, and regular worship in recognition of God's universal goodness to humanity.

2177,
2180-81     Sunday is observed as the primary holy day of obligation in the church. The faithful are required to participate in Mass on Sundays and other holy days of obligation.

2185-86     On Sundays and other holy days of obligation, Christians should abstain from any work or enterprise that inhibits the worship due to God. They should avoid everything that keeps them from devoting time and concern to serving the needs of their families and neighbors, especially the poor, the sick, and elderly. On Sunday, they should also refrain from those things that prevent necessary relaxation of mind and body.

## Commentary

This chapter begins with an affirmation of the inextricable connection between the two tablets of the decalogue, that is, between the first three commandments directed toward God and the remaining seven commandments which outline right conduct toward one's neighbor. This affirmation is important because it means that religious and moral obligations to God cannot be separated from moral obligations to other human beings. In developing this connection, the Catechism echoes the bible's emphasis on the social, relational dimension of religious and moral life, a dimension retrieved and highlighted by the Second Vatican Council.

In setting forth a foundation for moral conduct, however, the Catechism is not completely consistent. On the one hand, it situates the reception of the Ten Commandments in the context of the covenant between God and the Hebrews and characterizes the moral life as a response to God's loving initiative in humanity's personal and communal existence. On the other hand, the Catechism adopts a very different tone when it subordinates this affirmation of the social and relational foundation for morality to an emphasis on obedient acceptance of established moral laws and the duty to apply these commandments at all times and in all circumstances.

Following upon the decisions of Vatican II, this chapter of the Catechism affirms the right of religious liberty and offers an understanding picture of some forms of atheism. Religious liberty is described as the natural right to decide one's religious affiliation and to hold one's religious convictions without interference or hindrance from political authorities. This respect for religious liberty was a decisive development at Vatican II, overturning the previous insistence upon the special privileges of the Roman Catholic Church. It should be noted, however, that the

Catechism does not state that religious liberty is an unlimited right or that this right exists within the church itself. Some have criticized the church for insisting on respect from the state for the religious convictions of individual believers while failing to respect believers within the church who hold religious convictions different from the official, non-infallible teaching of the hierarchical magisterium.

The Catechism reaffirms the conviction of Vatican II that some forms of atheism are not as culpable as others. Believers themselves are identified as one of the causes of contemporary atheism insofar as their religious or moral life sometimes gives little evidence of their life in God. Believers are also held responsible for contributing to atheism to the extent that they present to others a deficient picture of God. Contemporary theologians, such as Karl Rahner, have developed these ideas further and have placed them in the context of a comprehensive theological anthropology, that is, a comprehensive, theological interpretation of the human person. The foundation of Rahner's anthropology is the conviction that people are by nature made to be in relation to God. Building upon this foundation, he explains how some people can reject God in their explicit words, while affirming God implicitly in their manner of living. He also explains how—contrary to popular opinion—the freedom to be authentically human increases rather than decreases with the recognition and incorporation of God into people's lives. Attention to contemporary theology's fuller discussion of the distinction between culpable and inculpable atheism and the distinction between explicit and anonymous Christianity can enrich the reading of the Catechism's explication of the first commandment.

It is significant that in its explanation of the meaning of the third commandment the Catechism broadens the obligations entailed by it. The Catechism affirms the religious celebration of Sunday as a moral commandment. It adds, however, that relaxation of mind and body; service to the sick, infirm, and elderly; and family time together are also obligations that flow from the commandment to keep holy the sabbath.

## Suggested Readings

Second Vatican Council. "Dignitatis Humanae: Declaration on Religious Freedom." *Vatican II: The Conciliar and Post-conciliar Documents.* Austin Flannery, ed. Boston: St. Paul Books, 1989.

_____. "Gaudium et Spes: Pastoral Constitution on the Church in the Modern World." *Vatican II: The Conciliar and Post-conciliar Documents.* Austin Flannery, ed. Boston: St. Paul Books, 1989.

# Chapter Two:
# You Shall Love Your Neighbor
### (n. 2196-2557)

## Summary

This chapter discusses the moral obligations included in love of one's neighbor. The topics covered in this discussion are quite far-ranging. The explication of the fourth commandment, for example, includes a description of the proper attitude toward civil authorities and the responsibility of society for the well-being of families. The treatment of the fifth commandment includes consideration of capital punishment, euthanasia and extraordinary medical procedures, just war, and peace. In explaining the sixth commandment the text includes a discussion of homosexuality and modern medical techniques for overcoming sterility. The seventh commandment becomes the context in which to consider social justice, the equitable distribution of the world's resources, and workers' rights as well as stealing and fairness. After explaining the evils of false speech, including the ills of propaganda, the section on the eighth commandment explains the necessity of truth and beauty in sacred art. The ninth commandment praises purity and condemns lust, even when it remains within one's heart. The tenth warns against greed and envy, and applauds detachment.

*Love your neighbor as yourself (n. 2196)*

2196    The fourth through the tenth commandments are
        summed up in these words: "Love your neighbor as
        yourself."

*The Fourth Commandment: Honor your father and your mother.*
*(n. 2197-2256)*

2197,   The fourth commandment applies primarily to the re-
2199    lationship between children and their parents. After
        God people should honor their parents, to whom they
        owe the gift of life and who have passed on to them
        the knowledge of God.

2201,   Marriage, which is based on the equal dignity of the
2203    partners and the mutual consent of the spouses, is in-
        tended to promote the good of the spouses and the
        procreation and education of children.

2204-05 The Christian family can be called a "domestic church"
        because faith, hope, and love are nurtured in the home
        and shared with others.

2207,   Family life provides an initiation to life in society. For
2209-11 this reason, society has a particular responsibility to
        support and strengthen the family. Society's obliga-
        tions to the family include assuring the right to bring
        up children in accordance with the parents' religious
        and moral convictions, the right to obtain work and
        lodging, and the right to medical care and security.

2216-18 Children owe their parents respect. For children living
        at home with their parents, this respect includes obedi-
        ence to every parental demand that is motivated by
        concern for the well-being of the child or the family.
        Although obedience toward parents ceases with the
        child's emancipation upon reaching the age of major-

ity, adult children continue to owe respect to their parents and they ought, to the best of their ability, give them material and moral assistance in old age and in times of illness or distress.

Parents have the duty to respect their children and to educate them. This parental duty includes the responsibility to create a stable home environment in which loving kindness, forgiveness, mutual cooperation and service, and religious faith are nurtured.            2221-27

Parents should not constrain adult children in their choice of a profession or in their choice of a spouse. Parents should teach their children that the Christian's first vocation is to follow Jesus.            2230, 2232

The fourth commandment applies secondarily to all relationships among family members and to all relationships involving legitimate authorities such as leaders, teachers, and the like. The fourth commandment requires people to honor those who, for the wellbeing of people and society, have received authority from God.            2197, 2199, 2234

To exercise authority in society means to serve the common good and the needs of others.            2235

Political authorities are obliged to respect the fundamental rights of the human person.            2237

Citizens are obliged to work with civil authorities in promoting society's well-being. At times conscience may require citizens to protest against those actions of civil authorities which are harmful to the dignity of persons and the good of the community.            2238-39, 2242

Although the church is not to be identified with any political party or society, the church has the right to            2246

105

pass moral judgments, even in matters of politics, when the fundamental rights of individuals or the salvation of souls are involved.

*The Fifth Commandment: You shall not murder.*
*(n. 2257-2330)*

2258,
2261     No human being can claim the right to destroy directly an innocent human being. God alone is the Lord of life. The law forbidding the willful murder of an innocent person is universally valid.

2264     Legitimate self-defense is a right based on authentic self-love. Those who defend their lives are not guilty of homicide even if they must use deadly force against the aggressor.

2265     Legitimate defense not only can be a right, but also a serious duty for those who are responsible for others' lives or the common good of family or state.

2266-67  To the extent that human lives can be defended against aggressors and the public peace protected by means other than the death penalty and military force, such non-violent measures are preferable. The death penalty, however, is not ruled out in cases of extreme gravity.

2269     The fifth commandment prohibits both exposing anyone to mortal risk without serious reason and refusing to help anyone in danger. For example, the fifth commandment obliges people to take reasonable steps to alleviate a deadly famine.

2270     Human life must be respected and protected from the moment of conception until death.

2271-72  Abortion willed as an end in itself is seriously contrary to the moral law. Similarly, it is not permissible to have or perform an abortion even for a presumably good end. The church punishes this sin against human life with the canonical penalty of excommunication.

The human embryo must be treated as a person from conception and must be cared for and protected. Certain medical procedures are not to be allowed: for example, non-therapeutic attempts to influence the genetic inheritance of the embryo (sex-selection) or the production of human embryos for the purpose of being used as disposable "biological material."    2274-75

Direct euthanasia—an action or omission which, in and of itself or in its intention, causes the death of a handicapped, sick, or dying person—is morally unacceptable.    2277

The fifth commandment, however, does not oblige people to continue medical procedures that are unnecessarily burdensome, dangerous, extraordinary, or disproportionate to the hoped-for results.    2278

Because people are stewards, not owners, of the life God has entrusted to them, they may not commit suicide.    2280

Because physical life and health are precious gifts from God, people must take reasonable care of themselves. Society must assist people in obtaining conditions that permit growth and development: food, clothing, housing, health care, basic education, and employment or social assistance.    2288

Medical or scientific experiments on human beings are not morally legitimate if they expose the subject's life or physical and psychological integrity to disproportionate or avoidable risks. Organ transplants, for example, are morally acceptable, even meritorious,    2295-96 if the physical and psychological dangers incurred by the living donor are proportionate to the good sought for the recipient.

2297      The fifth commandment condemns kidnapping, taking hostages, acts of terrorism, torture, and the mutilation or sterilization of innocent persons for non-therapeutic reasons.

2302-03      The fifth commandment, according to its interpretation by Jesus, also forbids wrath (the desire for vengeance that involves deliberately seeking to kill or seriously wound another) and hatred (wishing evil on another).

2307      The fifth commandment urges the establishment of peace and the avoidance of war.

2304      Peace is more than the absence of war. It involves respect for the dignity of individuals and nations, loving solidarity with others, and justice.

2308-09      Because of the evils and injustices that accompany every war, people and nations must do whatever is reasonably possible to avoid war. Defense of one's nation by military force is morally legitimate only when the conditions of the church's "just war" teaching have been strictly met.

2312-14      Even in a just war, there are certain actions that are not morally permissible. For example, every operation of war that aims indiscriminately at the destruction of whole cities or widespread areas, together with their inhabitants, is immoral.

2315      The arms race does not assure peace, but risks aggravating the causes of war. In addition, the arms race impedes the human, social, and economic development of peoples.

People must work to remove from the world injustice 2317
and excessive inequality in the economic and social order because they threaten peace and cause wars.

*The Sixth Commandment: You shall not commit adultery.*
*(n. 2331-2399)*

According to the church's tradition, the sixth command- 2336
ment encompasses the whole of human sexuality.

Because women and men are equally created in the di- 2334-35
vine image, every woman and man has equal personal
dignity, and each of the sexes images both divine power and divine loving kindness.

Sexuality affects all aspects of the human person, and 2332-33
every woman and man is called to recognize and accept her or his sexual identity.

All Christians are called to lives of chastity in ac- 2348-49
cordance with their state in life, whether married, single, or religiously celibate.

Chastity means the successful integration of sexuality 2337-43
within the person. It involves temperance and self-
control, which is a gradual and lifelong process.

Among the sins seriously contrary to the virtue of 2351-56
chastity are lust, masturbation, fornication, por-
nography, prostitution, and rape.

Although homosexual acts are contrary to the natural 2357-58
moral law, people who experience homosexual ten-
dencies must be accepted with respect, compassion,
and sensitivity.

Physical intimacy within marriage is a pledge of spir- 2360-61
itual communion and an integral part of marital love.

2363,    The twofold end of marriage is the good of the spouses
2366     and the transmission of life. This connection between
         the unitive and procreative aspects of marriage is not
         to be broken.

2368,    Although the sexual intercourse of married couples
2370     must remain open to the transmission of life, re-
         sponsible parenthood does not rule out the regulation
         of births.

2375-77  Scientific research aimed at reducing human sterility is
         to be encouraged, but those techniques that separate
         the sexual act from the procreative act are morally ob-
         jectionable.

2380-81, Adultery, polygamy, incest, and sexual intimacy be-
2387-91  tween unmarried persons are serious offenses against
         the dignity of marriage.

2382-86  Divorce is immoral because it breaks the contract and
         covenant to which the spouses freely consented. There
         is, however, an important difference between a spouse
         who has tried to be faithful to the sacrament of mar-
         riage and a spouse who, by a serious fault on his or her
         part, betrays a canonically valid marriage.

*The Seventh Commandment: You shall not steal.*
*(n. 2400-2463)*

2401     The seventh commandment requires justice and love in
         the stewardship of earthly goods and the fruits of hu-
         man labor.

2402-05  Although the earth and its resources are divided
         among all people so as to assure their security, the
         goods of creation ultimately belong to the whole hu-
         man race.

Every unjust taking away and keeping the goods of an-          2409
other is contrary to the seventh commandment. This
means that not only obvious cases of theft, but also cases of fraud, the payment of unjust wages, badly done
work, and waste are immoral.

The seventh commandment forbids acts or enterprises          2414
which, for any reason, lead to the enslavement of people.

Human dominion over animals and inanimate re-          2415-18
sources is not absolute. It must be tempered by concern for the quality of life of one's neighbors, including
generations to come. People must also respect creation's integrity, including the demand that animals not
be made to suffer needlessly or have their lives wasted.

The church makes moral judgments about economic          2420
and social matters when the fundamental rights of persons or the salvation of souls requires it.

The church's social teaching rejects both totalitarian          2423-25
and atheistic ideologies (associated in modern times
with communism or socialism) and individualism and
the absolute primacy of the "law of the marketplace"
over human labor (associated with modern capitalism).

Work is a human duty by which people share in the          2427-28
work of creation. It can be a means of sanctification
and a renewal of earthly realities. All people should be
able to derive from their work the means to provide
for their own lives and the lives of their dependents.

The seventh commandment requires that access to jobs          2433-34
and professions be open to all without unjust discrimination, and that all workers receive a just wage
for their labor.

2437-40   On the international level the seventh commandment requires solidarity, justice, and love. This means that international economic and financial institutions must be reformed to promote fairer relations between rich, well-developed nations and poor, less-advanced nations.

2444-47   Aiding the poor, spiritually and materially, is one of the chief witnesses to authentic love of neighbor. Providing such aid is often a demand of justice.

2448      Those who are oppressed by poverty are the object of the church's preferential love, which works for the poor's relief, defense, and liberation.

*The Eighth Commandment: You shall not bear false witness against your neighbor. (n. 2464-2513)*

2464-65   Since God is truthful and the source of all truth, God's people are called to live in the truth. The eighth commandment forbids misrepresenting the truth in all relations with others.

2469      Truthfulness maintains a just balance between what ought to be expressed and what ought to be kept secret; it involves both honesty and discretion.

2477-79   Respect for the reputation of others rules out every attitude and word likely to cause them unjust harm, including rash judgment, detraction, and calumny.

2482-83,  Lying is the most direct offense against the truth.
2488      Lying is speaking a falsehood with the intention of deceiving someone who has the right to know the truth.

2487      Every offense against truth and justice, including offenses against the reputation of others, demands restitution.

Sometimes the good and security of others, or respect for privacy and the common good, might require an individual to remain silent about certain matters or to use discreet language. 2488-89

Because society has a right to information based on truth, freedom, justice, and solidarity, neither the communications media nor governments ought to disseminate false information with the intent of manipulating public opinion. 2494, 2497-98

Truth can also be expressed in works of art. The fine arts, in particular sacred art, are oriented toward the infinite beauty of God. 2501-02

*The Ninth Commandment: Neither shall you covet your neighbor's wife. (n. 2514-2533)*

The ninth commandment forbids indulgence in carnal concupiscence, that is, intense sexual desire that inclines individuals to sin. 2514-15

Jesus' interpretation of the ninth commandment encourages purity of heart, which consists in bringing people's minds and wills into conformity with God's holiness, as it is expressed in charity, chastity, and love of truth. 2517-18

Purity calls for modesty and decency in words, actions, and dress. 2521-25

*The Tenth Commandment: Neither shall you desire your neighbor's house, or field, or male or female slave, or ox, or donkey, or anything that belongs to your neighbor. (n. 2534-2557)*

Whereas the ninth commandment addresses the concupiscence of the flesh, the tenth commandment addresses the concupiscence of the heart. 2534

2535-36    A person's natural desire for pleasant things becomes sinful when it does not obey reasonable moderation and leads to coveting unjustly what belongs to or is due to others.

2539       When people wish serious harm to others in order to appropriate their possessions for themselves, their envy has become mortally sinful.

2544-47    Jesus calls on his disciples to detach themselves from riches and to be poor in spirit so that they can enter the kingdom of heaven.

2548       Desire for true happiness delivers people from immoderate attachment to this world's goods and finds its fulfillment in the vision of God.

## Commentary

The range of issues dealt with in this chapter of the Catechism is extremely broad. They include relations between family and government, sexual morality, war and peace, civil disobedience, and just wages. Despite this wide range of issues, some characteristics consistently appear in the treatment of these topics. The principles of the inherent dignity and the social nature of the human person underlie this entire section on morality. In addition, this chapter of the Catechism follows the traditional practice of official church teaching on moral issues: It formulates clear material norms to be obeyed in all the diverse areas of human conduct. The Catechism, however, often expands the traditional interpretation of the commandments to include less obvious violations of the commandments. Greater attention is paid to the social dimension of the Christian life, and the spirit of the law is considerably broadened.

Examples of this increased attention to the social dimension can be found in the Catechism's explanation of the fourth and fifth commandments. In its explication of the fourth commandment, the Catechism reminds Catholics that they have an obligation to work with government in promoting the well-being of society, and that the church in its role as a moral authority has the right to make judgments about political and social matters as they impact families and society. Correlatively, the Catechism reminds society that it has an obligation to insure the rights of the family in obtaining work, housing, and medical care. In defining the scope of the fifth commandment, the Catechism claims that if society fails to assist people in obtaining conditions that permit human growth and development—food, housing, health care, education, and employment or social assistance—it violates the commandment against murder.

Examples of the broadening of the scope of the commandments can be seen clearly in the presentation of the seventh commandment. The failure of an employer to pay a just wage and the failure of an employee to do good work are both regarded as violations of the prohibition against stealing. The meaning of the seventh commandment is further broadened to include some ecological considerations. The Catechism reminds people to use the world's natural resources wisely out of a sense of moral obligation to future generations and a sense of profound respect for God's creation. Similarly, the Catechism moderates past interpretations of the biblical reference to human dominion over the rest of creation by insisting that this dominion is not absolute and that animals ought not to be made to suffer needlessly or have their lives wasted.

Sexual morality is treated under the fifth, sixth, and ninth commandments. The Catechism begins its consideration of this important and often controverted area of human existence with the recognition that, due to the fact that sexuality affects all aspects of people's lives, every person is called to accept her or his sexual identity. This healthy need for the recognition of one's sexual identity applies to all people, regardless of their chosen state of life: single, married, or religiously celibate. In this framework which extols the goodness of human sexuality, the Catechism demands respect for people who have a homosexual identity, while continuing to uphold the church's traditional condemnation of homosexual acts.

The affirmation that men and women are equally created in the divine image is the second affirmation that contributes to the foundation of the Catechism's discussion of sexual morality. The Catechism, in a positive and important move, alerts its readers to the danger of gender stereotypes by refusing to identify men as the exclusive or primary image of divine power and women as the exclusive or primary image of divine love and tenderness. Rather, the Catechism declares that each gender images both divine power and divine loving kindness.

Despite these positive elements in the discussion of sexual morality, some moral theologians will criticize the Catechism for not treating sexual and social matters equally. They point out that over the last thirty years the teaching of the hierarchical magisterium on matters of war and peace, economic justice, and politics has shown itself to be flexible and sensitive to historical context. These pronouncements have also expressed an openness to a greater role for the individual's own discernment of what is good. This flexibility, sensitivity, and openness, however, is not apparent in the teaching of the hierarchical magisterium on matters of sexuality. Sexual intimacy outside of marriage, artificial contraception, masturbation, and divorce consistently continue to be condemned as morally illicit.

Some theologians explain the difference in official teaching on social and sexual matters in terms of the ethical model underlying the teaching. Whereas the hierarchical magisterium has been more open to using a relational-responsible model in its recent social teaching, it has been less willing to use this model in its sexual teaching. Instead, it continues to use a legal model in sexual matters. When a legal model is used, there is very little gray area in moral decision making. If something is against the law, it is morally wrong; if it is not against the law, it is morally acceptable. When, on the other hand, a relational-responsible model is used, there is considerably more gray area because one must ask additional questions besides "What is the law?" One must also ask about the disposition of the moral agent, the circumstances in which the moral decision is to be made, and one's relationship to the other person or persons involved, and then one must give serious consideration to the answers to these questions.

No moral theologian has had a greater influence in changing

the orientation of contemporary Catholic moral theology than Bernard Häring, a Redemptorist priest who taught moral theology for many years in Rome and who helped develop several documents of the Second Vatican Council. In the twenty-five years between the publication of his landmark work, *The Law of Christ* (1954), and his *Free and Faithful in Christ* (1978), Häring influenced a generation of moral theologians to adopt a more biblical, personalist, inductive, and creative approach to ethics.

Over the past thirty years increasing numbers of moral theologians, following Häring's lead, have called on church leaders to integrate a more historically conscious, more relation-oriented approach into official church teachings about marriage and divorce, artificial contraception, and other issues of sexual morality. Moral theologians today often appeal to recent developments in official church teaching on social matters to support their proposals for changes in official teaching on sexual matters.

The encyclicals of Pope John XXIII recognize the fact that attention must be given to the specific historical context in which the moral decision is made. In *Mater et Magistra* (1961), Pope John XXIII notes that, in the thirty years that had elapsed since Pope Pius XI's social encyclical (*Quadragesimo Anno*), the economic scene had changed radically. And in each of the four major sections of *Pacem in Terris* (1963), the pope devoted attention to what he called "the signs of the times," that is, the historical characteristics of the present day, before making his pastoral recommendations for peace.

Pope Paul VI not only continued, but also enlarged the attention given to the historical context in his apostolic letter *Octogesima Adveniens* (1971). Before addressing the new social problems of the 1970s, Pope Paul VI admitted that it was difficult to put forward a solution that had universal validity. He believed that the social situations around the world were so different that Christian individuals and communities would have to discern for themselves the appropriate options and just commitments to which the gospel was calling them (see *Octogesima Adveniens,* #4). This affirmation of the freedom and responsibility of individuals to make moral decisions reflects the recognition that situations are diverse and often ambiguous. It accepts the fact that people can come to legitimate and valid, yet different moral conclusions about what is to be done in certain situations.

This flexibility in social teaching is evident in the pastoral letters of the U.S. Catholic bishops on war and peace (*The Challenge of Peace*, 1983) and on the economy (*Economic Justice for All*, 1986). On the question of whether it is morally permissible to engage in war or not, the bishops clearly describe two different and permissible options for the individual: to engage in war only if the war is justified (the just-war theory) or never to engage in war (pacifism). In this pastoral, the individual is reminded of the general moral principles that apply in all situations (for example, the dignity of every human being, the impermissibility of directly intending to kill non-combatants), but the choice to be made within the parameters of those general principles is left to the conscientious decision of the individual.

The Catechism shows this type of flexibility on certain topics, but not in all areas of morality. Concerning the use of lethal force, the Catechism declares that non-violent responses to crime are preferred, yet it does not rule out the use of capital punishment in cases of extreme gravity. Consquently, Catholics who endorse the use of the death penalty in serious cases as well as Catholics who oppose it in every case can both recognize themselves as being faithful to the teaching of the Catechism. In a similar fashion, when it addresses the question of an appropriate economic system for society, the Catechism endorses neither communism and socialism, nor individualism and capitalism. It makes the point that there are certain important values or principles in each of these different systems, but that no socioeconomic system, taken by itself as it currently exists, provides a perfectly adequate resolution of the economic and social needs of the individual vis-à-vis society and vice versa.

This openness or flexibility is generally not evident in the Catechism's treatment of sexual matters. It categorically condemns abortion, masturbation, homosexual acts, and artificial means of contraception. It also singles out abortion from other forms of killing as an act that incurs the penalty of excommunication from the Roman Catholic Church.

Although moral theologians may affirm the formal norms or basic values underlying the specific prohibitions related to matters of sexuality—for example, the sanctity of life or the sacredness of heterosexual intimacy—some moral theologians claim that these values cannot be transformed into exceptionless moral laws. They insist that the church's sexual teaching needs to balance its attention to the act performed with attention to the particular individual performing the act. This means bringing the specifics of the situation, the intention and disposition of the agent, the quality of the relationship, and modern psychological and medical knowledge about the human person into reflection upon the morality of human sexual behavior in a more substantive manner. Reading the reflections of contemporary moral theologians on sexual matters can not only illuminate the complexity of moral decision making in such matters, but also explain why differences in judgment in these matters are often sharp and heated.

Reading some contemporary theological reflections about marriage can enrich the Catechism's discussion of divorce. The Catechism describes divorce as a serious offense against the natural law, and it consequently labels divorce as immoral. Although the text notes that there is a difference between a spouse who is the innocent victim of a civil divorce and a spouse who directly causes a canonically valid marriage to fail, the Catechism does not incorporate into its teaching new insights gained from psychology and from theological reflection upon the spiritual dimension of marriage. Theologians who have incorporated these new insights into their work ask whether all marriages that meet the traditional criteria for sacramental marriages are, in fact, authentically sacramental and indissoluble.

Instead of regarding marriage as a *contract* that becomes indissoluble and sacramental when freely consented to by baptized Christians on the day of their wedding and sexually consummated subsequently, some theologians speak of marriage as an ongoing commitment to a lifelong, *covenantal* relationship of Christian love. Such a relationship requires a maturity of person and a maturity of faith that many baptized Christians lack.

This raises the question of whether a baptized Christian who has no genuine religious convictions or who has limited personal maturity can genuinely enter in a sacramental marriage. The church, particularly in the United States, has expended much time and energy in pastoral ministry to divorced Catholics and to remarried Catholics. The pastoral challenge of being simultaneously a community of healing and forgiveness while insisting on the sanctity and permanence of sacramental marriage is inadequately reflected in the Catechism's brief treatment of divorce.

Part Two of the Catechism (numbers 1601-1666) sheds additional light on the church's understanding of marriage when it considers matrimony in the context of the seven sacraments.

## Suggested Readings

Cahill, Lisa Sowle. *Between the Sexes: Foundations for a Christian Ethics of Sexuality*. Minneapolis: Augsburg Fortress, 1985.

_____. *Women and Sexuality*. Mahwah, NJ: Paulist Press, 1992.

Curran, Charles E., and Richard A. McCormick, eds. *Readings in Moral Theology, No. 8: Dialogue about Catholic Sexual Teaching*. Mahwah, NJ: Paulist Press, 1993.

Genovesi, Vincent J. *In Pursuit of Love: Catholic Morality and Human Sexuality*. Collegeville, MN: Liturgical Press, 1987.

Hanigan, James P. *What Are They Saying About Sexual Morality?* Mahwah, NJ: Paulist Press, 1982.

Nelson, James B. *Embodiment: An Approach to Sexuality and Christian Theology*. Minneapolis: Augsburg Fortress, 1979.

# PART FOUR

# CHRISTIAN PRAYER

# Part Four:
# Christian Prayer

**Summary**

This part explains the role of prayer in the Christian life. Prayer is presented as the means to respond to God's initiative in people's lives and as the means of maintaining a relationship with God. Without a relationship with God, the Christian life is impossible. Section One of Part Four discusses the role of prayer in the Christian life as well as the sources and types of prayer. Section Two offers a detailed explanation of the Lord's Prayer.

# Section One:
# Prayer in the Christian Life

**Summary**

Chapter One of Section One begins with a brief history of prayer, and devotes special attention to the development of prayer in the Hebrew Scriptures and to Jesus' own example of prayer. It concludes with an explanation of the five forms of prayer. Chapter Two briefly describes the Christian tradition of prayer. Special emphasis is given to the Holy Spirit as the interior teacher of the many and varied forms of Christian prayer and spirituality. Chapter Three describes vocal prayer, meditation, and mental prayer. It also addresses the difficulties people encounter in trying to pray and suggests effective means to counteract those difficulties.

### Christian Prayer (n. 2558-2565)

Prayer can be defined as the ascent of the mind to God    2258-59
or the request for suitable blessings from God. In a
more general sense, it is the means people use to sustain their relationship with God.

Prayer arises in response to God's free promise of sal-    2561,
vation. God's initiative of love comes first; the human    2567
response of prayer follows.

In the terminology of the Bible, prayer originates in the    2562-63
human heart, the hidden center of the person known
fully only by God.

# Chapter One:
# The Revelation of Prayer
### (n. 2566-2649)

God has always called people to relationship with    2566-67,
God's self. All religions give evidence of humanity's    2569
search for God and their response to God's initiative.

In the Hebrew Scriptures, prayer is bound up with hu-    2568
man history because God's relationship to the people
is worked out in historical events.

The example of Abraham shows that the attentiveness    2570
of the human heart to the divine will is essential to
prayer.

| 2574, 2577 | Moses' prayer, after the people had turned away from God despite their deliverance from slavery in Egypt, gives one of the most striking examples of intercessory prayer. |

| 2581 | The temple of Jerusalem eventually became the place where God's people learned the various ways of praying. |

| 2581, 2584 | The Hebrew prophets warned people of the danger of external worship and called them to inner conversion and conversation with God. The prophets interceded with God for their people. |

| 2585 | From the time of David to the time of Jesus, the Hebrew Scriptures show a deepening in personal prayer and in prayer for others. |

| 2586 | Although they derive from the communities of the Holy Land and the Diaspora, the psalms embrace all of creation. The psalms commemorate the promises God has already fulfilled and they direct people's minds and hearts to the final fulfillment of God's saving actions. |

| 2589 | The psalms disclose the spontaneity and simplicity of prayer as well as the burdens and trials of those who pray the psalms. |

| 2600, 2604 | Jesus' manner of praying reveals the need to pray before decisive moments in life as well as the need to commit one's self with trust to God's will. Jesus' prayers begin with thanksgiving to God. They teach people how to ask for blessing from God: Before the gift is given, the people offering the prayer need to commit themselves to the Giver. |

| 2608 | According to the testimony of the gospels, Jesus em- |

phasized inner conversion as a necessary component of authentic prayer. He insisted on reconciliation with one's brother or sister before presenting an offering on the altar. He urged his disciples to love their enemies and to pray for their persecutors.

Jesus teaches people to pray with filial commitment to God and with boldness. He also teaches something new: to pray in his name.                   2609-10, 2614

After the death and resurrection of Jesus, the Holy Spirit teaches the Christian community and forms it in the life of prayer, guiding it in new formulations of traditional prayer forms.                   2623

Five forms of prayer, revealed in the canonical scriptures, have become normative for Christians: blessing and adoration, petition, intercession, thanksgiving, and praise.                   2625

In the prayer of blessing, people respond gratefully to God's gifts of blessing. In the prayer of adoration, they acknowledge themselves as creatures before God and exalt in the greatness of God's creative and redemptive activity.                   2626-28

In the prayer of petition, people acknowledge their dependence on God. After first asking divine forgiveness for their sinfulness, the prayer of petition focuses on the desire for the coming of God's kingdom.                   2629-32

In the prayer of intercession, people ask for divine mercy on behalf of others. This includes praying not only for friends, but also for enemies.                   2634-36

In the prayer of thanksgiving, people give thanks, together with Christ, for all the events of their lives.                   2637-38

2639    In the prayer of praise, people sing of God's glory, not for what God has done, but simply because God exists. This form of prayer embraces the other forms and brings them all to God.

2643    The eucharist contains and expresses all five forms of prayer.

# Chapter Two:
# The Tradition of Prayer
## (n. 2650-2696)

2650    It is not enough to wait for prayer to arise spontaneously from the human heart or to have an intellectual understanding of what the Bible reveals about prayer. One must also want to pray and to learn how to pray. The Holy Spirit, active in the tradition of Christian prayer, teaches people how to pray.

2653,   Among the sources of Christian prayer are the Word of
2656-58  God, the liturgy of the church, and the virtues of faith, hope, and love. The preeminent source of prayer is love.

2664    All Christian prayer, whether individual or communal, is addressed primarily to God the Father in the name of Jesus.

2665-66,  All the liturgical traditions of the church include
2668    prayer addressed to Christ. The name "Jesus" (meaning "God saves") is the only name that contains the presence it signifies. Invoking the name of Jesus is the simplest way of praying.

2672    Although there are as many ways to pray as there are

126

people, the Holy Spirit, who is the interior teacher of Christian prayer, acts in all and with all.

Because of Mary's special cooperation with the work-                    2675
ing of the Holy Spirit, the church developed the tradi-
tion of praying to and with Mary.

The witnesses to Christian faith who have gone before                   2683
us, especially the saints, share in the living tradition of
prayer by the example of their lives and their prayer.
The Christian community today can ask for their intercession.

The rich diversity of Christian spiritualities contributes              2684
to the living tradition of prayer and offers important
guides for the spiritual life.

The Christian family is the first place where in-                       2685
dividuals learn to pray and to be attentive to the action
of the Holy Spirit.

The catechesis of both children and adults aims at                      2688
teaching them to meditate on God's word, to par-
ticipate in the liturgical prayer of the community, and
to interiorize God's word always.

The choice of a suitable place for prayer is important.                 2691

# Chapter Three:
# The Life of Prayer
## (n. 2697-2758)

In order to help people pray and remember God, the                    2697-98
church offers certain traditional rhythms of praying.
These include daily prayer, prayer before and after
meals, Sunday eucharist, and the liturgical cycle.

2699    Although people respond differently to God in prayer, the Christian tradition has developed three privileged expressions of prayer: vocal prayer, meditation, and mental prayer.

2701-04   Vocal prayer expresses the natural human need to express one's feelings and interior prayer externally. Vocal prayer, which is the form of prayer most accessible to all people, follows Jesus' example and prepares them for contemplation.

2705-08   Although there are many different methods of meditation, they all express the human desire to understand what God is asking of people in their own situation. Christian meditation, which focuses primarily on the mysteries of Christ, makes use of thought, imagination, and emotion in order to deepen one's faith and transform a person's heart to follow Christ.

2709,     Mental prayer, which is the simplest expression of
2712-18   prayer, involves an interior interchange between God and the human heart. In mental prayer, Christians focus on Jesus and are silently united with him in his own prayer.

2725    Although prayer is a gift of grace, it is also a human response requiring effort. Just as it is a struggle to live the Christian life, so too it is a struggle to pray and maintain union with God.

2726-27   The struggle of prayer involves confronting mistaken notions about prayer (for example, that prayer is merely a psychological need or that it is incompatible with mundane, daily activities) and resisting the falsely scientistic, rationalistic, and utilitarian presuppositions of modern culture that can undermine the value and importance of prayer.

Distraction and dryness are two difficulties that are of-    2729-31
ten encountered in a life of prayer. Awareness of those
attachments that draw people away from God, a desire
to be vigilantly attentive to the movement of God in
one's life, and renewed faith can help individuals combat these difficulties.

Lack of faith, apathy, or sloth are common temptations    2732-35
in prayer. People can combat these temptations by ex-
amining their priorities in life, their motives for prayer,
and their image of God.

Sometimes when people think about prayer, they won-    2735-37
der whether God hears their petitions and whether
prayer is effective. In answering these questions, people need to ask themselves whether they regard God
as an instrument to be manipulated by prayer and
whether they ask God for suitable blessings.

Faith teaches that it is always possible to pray, that    2743-45
prayer is vitally important, and that prayer and the
Christian life cannot be separated.

Jesus' final prayer (see John's Gospel, Chapter 17)    2746-51
sums up the whole plan of creation and salvation, inspires the petitions of the Lord's Prayer, and reveals
knowledge of the indivisible union of Father and Son.

## Commentary

Part Four is the shortest of the four parts in the Catechism. In the
early drafts this section was an epilogue to the three major parts
of the Catechism. It was quite brief and consisted of an explanation of the Lord's Prayer. By the time the Catechism was completed in 1992, however, the part on prayer had been expanded
in response to the criticisms of bishops and theologians who had
reviewed the provisional drafts of the text. The material was no
longer identified as an epilogue, but was given equal status to
the other three major divisions of the Catechism. The com-

mentary on the Lord's Prayer was augmented with a new section detailing the development of the tradition of prayer in the Christian life.

One might well expect that the majority of Catholics, if they had been consulted, would have strongly endorsed the expansion of this section because prayer occupies a more prominent position in the experience and everyday life of believers than does a detailed explanation of the different elements of the creed as found in Part One of the Catechism.

Among the positive and noteworthy features of Part Four, one could mention its initial situating of prayer within the context of the natural human desire for God and the overarching biblical orientation of its exposition of the development of prayer.

Some of the other positive features of Section One could be further developed. For example, both in its discussion of the role of the Hebrew prophets and of Jesus in the development of prayer, the Catechism notes that prayer is not to become a mere external ritual, but is to spring from an inner conversion to God. It refers to Jesus' insistence that reconciliation with one's brother or sister is necessary before one offers worship to God, yet it fails to develop more explicitly this connection between prayer and loving action on behalf of one's neighbor. As we have already observed with regard to Chapter Two (*The Human Community*) of Section One of Part Three, the Catechism does refer to commitment to social justice as part of the Christian life, but it does not fully develop there the connection between religious faith and social action, just as it does not fully develop here the connection between prayer and commitment to addressing the needs of one's neighbors.

Similarly, the Catechism rightly acknowledges the diversity of spiritualities within the Christian tradition and affirms their contribution to the life of the church. One wishes, however, that this acknowledgment had been broadened into a description of some of the more influential forms of spirituality and an identification of their appropriateness to the different needs and personalities of individuals.

Reference to the life and work of Thomas Merton, the Trappist monk who inspired the spiritual life of a generation of Christians both before and after his death in 1968, would have been most instructive at this point. In his life and spirituality, Merton made a firm connection between religious faith and social concern. Although adopting the life of a hermit at the abbey of Our Lady of Gethsemani in Kentucky, he grounded his contemplative life in social concern. He also explored diverse spiritual resources in his quest to find God through prayer. Although a Catholic Christian, he explored Eastern spirituality for ways to enhance his own spiritual life.

Contemporary theology, in its retrieval of previously neglected spiritual resources and in its re-thinking of the relationship between divine and human activity in shaping human history, provides some interesting insights that go beyond those contained in the Catechism. Although it refers to Thomas Aquinas, John of the Cross, Ignatius of Loyola, and other esteemed spiritual writers from the Middle Ages in its description of the development of prayer traditions, the Catechism tends to draw predominantly from the ancient male authors of the so-called patristic period. Of the many women who made significant contributions to enrich the prayer life of the church, it makes mention only of Teresa of Avila and Thérèse of Lisieux. Theologians working in the field of spirituality today, by contrast, frequently draw upon the insights of Hildegard of Bingen, Julian of Norwich, and others in formulating a prayer life and spirituality that is fruitful for contemporary believers.

Contemporary theologians have also engaged in a re-thinking of the traditional understanding of divine providence. In dealing with the question of why people's prayers of petition sometimes seem not to be heard by God, the Catechism focuses on the inappropriate image of God that might underlie some of these petitions: that is, an image of God as an instrument to be manipulated for the fulfilment of personal desires. Although it is appropriate for the Catechism to observe, on the one hand, that the motivation for praying may at times be deficient and to affirm, on the other, that faith depends on an awareness of God's action in history, the Catechism fails to explain sufficiently the connection between what people ask God to do in prayer and what God intends to do by empowering people to use their freedom and responsibility to work on behalf of God's kingdom.

Insofar as contemporary theology attempts to overcome the temptation to human passivity and resignation that results from a traditional understanding of divine providence or pre-destination, it offers insights that can deepen and enrich the Catechism's exposition of the efficacy of prayer.

## Suggested Readings

Byrne, Lavinia, ed. *The Hidden Tradition: Women's Spiritual Writings Rediscovered.* New York: Crossroad, 1991.

Downey, Michael, ed. *The New Dictionary of Christian Spirituality.* Collegeville, MN: Liturgical Press (Glazier Books), 1993.

Egan, Harvey D. *Christian Mysticism: The Future of a Tradition.* Collegeville, MN: Liturgical Press (Pueblo Books), 1984.

Gutiérrez, Gustavo. *We Drink From Our Own Wells: The Spiritual Journey of a People.* Maryknoll, NY: Orbis Books, 1984.

Huebsch, Bill. *A New Look at Prayer: Searching for Bliss.* Mystic, CT: Twenty-Third Publications, 1991.

Lane, George. *Christian Spirituality: An Historical Sketch.* Chicago: Loyola University Press, 1984.

McGinn, Bernard, and J. Meyendorff, eds. *Christian Spirituality: Origins to the Twelfth Century.* New York: Crossroad, 1987.

Merton, Thomas. *The Seven Storey Mountain.* 1948; rpt. New York: Harcourt Brace, 1990.

_____. *Conjectures of a Guilty Bystander.* New York: Doubleday, 1968.

Mollenkott, Virginia. *The Divine Feminine.* New York: Crossroad, 1984.

Sobrino, Jon. *Spirituality of Liberation.* Maryknoll, NY: Orbis Books, 1988.

# Section Two:
# The Lord's Prayer

## Summary

Section Two of Part Four offers a detailed analysis of the mean-ing of the Lord's Prayer, which is described as the fundamental or basic Christian prayer. It describes the changes that can occur in people and in their relationships with others when they au-thentically pray the Lord's Prayer. It emphasizes the importance of uniting one's will with Christ's in praying and working for the growth of God's kingdom.

### The Lord's Prayer (n. 2759-2865)

In response to the disciples' request to be taught how to pray, Jesus entrusted them with the fundamental Christian prayer, the Our Father.                                    2759

This prayer summarizes the entire gospel and provides the general foundation upon which individual prayers and petitions stand.                                              2761

It is called the Lord's Prayer because it comes from the Lord Jesus who, as the model of prayer, gives people the words with which to pray to the Father. Jesus also gives the Spirit by whom these words become dynamically embodied in people.                                    2765-66

The Lord's Prayer has been the basic prayer of the church from its very beginning. Grounded in liturgical prayer, the Lord's Prayer has been an integral part of the divine office and the sacraments of initiation.     2767-69

The full meaning and power of the Lord's Prayer as the prayer of the whole church is revealed in the eucharistic liturgy.                                                2770

Simplicity, childlike trust, and humble yet joyous assurance are dispositions that characterize those who authentically pray the Our Father.                        2777-78

When people pray to God as Father, they must be sure to eliminate from their minds false paternal or maternal images. Because God transcends the categories of the created world, people are in danger of replacing the true God with an idol if they simplistically ascribe to God ideas drawn from worldly experience.            2779

2780,
2782
People can call on God as "Father" because Christ the Son has so revealed God and because God has adopted them as God's own children. The Lord's Prayer thus reveals people to themselves at the same time that it reveals God to them.

2784-85
Praying to God as a Father should develop two dispositions in people: the desire to become like God and the desire to become like children who trust their father.

2786-88
2790-93
When we say "our" Father, the adjective "our" signals two new relationships: a new relationship between an individual and God, in which God and the person belong to each other in love and faithfulness; and a new relationship among those who say this prayer, a relationship of unity and love that excludes no one and rejects division.

2794
"Who art in heaven" does not refer to a remote place, but to God's majesty and to God's presence in the hearts of the holy and just.

2803-04
The first three petitions of the Lord's Prayer (hallowed be thy name, thy kingdom come, thy will be done) acknowledge God's glory and pray for the coming of the divine kingdom and the fulfillment of the divine will.

2807-08
2813-14
The words "hallowed be Thy name" acknowledge God's holiness and ask that this divine holiness be continually recognized in people's lives and that it be accepted and affirmed by every nation and every person. God's name is made holy when people act rightly; it is blasphemed when people act wrongly.

2816,
2818-19
The words "Thy kingdom come" ask, through Christ's return, for the fulfillment of God's reign. They seek total righteousness, peace, and joy in the Holy Spirit (see Romans 14:17).

Although the growth of God's kingdom and the im-    2820
provement of society are distinct, they are not separate.
A person's orientation to eternal life does not lessen,
but reinforces his or her duty to serve justice and peace
in this world.

"Thy will be done on earth as it is in heaven" asks the    2825-26
Father to unite the will of the person saying the prayer
to his Son's will in order to fulfill the divine plan of salvation for the life of the world. People enter into God's
kingdom when they do God's will.

"Give us this day our daily bread" acknowledges God    2828-30
with trust as the source of life and all good things, both
material and spiritual. It is also a petition for the needs
of all people.

People misunderstand this fourth petition if they con-    2830-31,
clude that they should be idle and simply wait for God    2833-34
to give them their daily bread.  Rightly understood,
this petition means, on the one hand, that people
should not be overly anxious about their ability to provide for their own needs and, on the other hand, that
they must be responsive to the needs of the hungry
throughout the world.

Saying "forgive us our trespasses, as we forgive those    2839-40
who trespass against us" recognizes human sinfulness
before God and acknowledges that divine mercy will
penetrate people's hearts only to the extent that they
forgive those who have committed offenses against
them.

Forgiveness is a high point of Christian prayer. It is the    2844-45
fundamental condition for being reconciled with God
and with one another. It includes the forgiveness of
one's enemies.

2846    Praying "lead us not into temptation" asks God not to allow people to take the way that leads to sin, but to give them the discernment and strength to withstand trials and resist temptation.

2851,   Finally, "deliver us from evil" signifies asking to be de-
2854    livered from Satan and all present and future evils as well as to receive peace and perseverance while awaiting Christ's return.

## Commentary

Section Two of Part Four is a line-by-line reflection on the meaning of the Lord's Prayer. The Catechism's explanation of this fundamental Christian prayer is generally clear and straightforward; it is often inspiring and eloquent. It embodies not only many of the rich, past reflections on this prayer, but also incorporates some of the theological developments that have occurred since the Second Vatican Council in explaining the practical implications of praying the Lord's Prayer authentically.

In keeping with Vatican II and its retrieval of a biblical orientation, the Catechism affirms that worship of God and building up God's kingdom are intrinsically related. The Catechism states that God's name is hallowed (made holy) in people by their actions. Echoing Vatican II's *Pastoral Constitution on the Church in the Modern World*, it declares that the Christian orientation to eternal life does not lessen, but reinforces one's duty to serve justice and peace in this world.

Many theologians today take this basic affirmation of the social nature of prayer found in the Catechism and develop it more extensively. This is particularly the case with those theologians who are usually referred to as liberation theologians. They wish to overcome not only the past tendency of the church to disparage this world for the sake of the other world. They also wish to overturn the tendency to think of salvation in individualistic terms. The Catechism affirms this more communal and social understanding of the Christian life in its explication of the Lord's Prayer, just as it affirmed it in its explication of the moral life in Part Three. Contemporary theology develops these themes more extensively and cohesively, thereby complementing the pronouncements of the Catechism.

Another area in which contemporary theology can complement the Catechism is in its reflections about the image of God as Father. There is no denying that the fatherhood of God is an idea which can be traced back to Jesus himself and which has had a rich history in the subsequent tradition of the church. To its credit, the Catechism acknowledges the fact that culture and history influence the way people imagine God, and it reminds people that God transcends the categories of the created world. It does not go on, however, to develop this point. Neither does it consider how exclusively male images for God can have negative consequences for the self-image of women, nor does it consider how a fixation upon one particular image of God might eventually lead believers to falsely conclude that they now adequately comprehend the mystery of God with this one image. Contemporary theology, especially theology influenced by feminism, has expended considerable time, energy, and creativity in exploring this issue. Doing some reading in this contemporary theology can illuminate the importance of this issue as well as clarify the implications of the images people use to address God in prayer.

## Suggested Readings

Cunningham, Lawrence S. *Catholic Prayer*. New York: Crossroad, 1989.

Dorr, Donal. *Spirituality and Justice*. Maryknoll, NY: Orbis Books, 1984.

Galilea, Segundo. *Following Jesus*. Maryknoll, NY: Orbis Books, 1981.

Johnson, Elizabeth. *She Who Is*. New York: Crossroad, 1992.

McFague, Sallie. *Models of God*. Minneapolis: Augsburg Fortress, 1987.

Meehan, Francis X. *A Contemporary Social Spirituality*. Maryknoll, NY: Orbis Books, 1982.

# Conclusion

*The Catechism: Highlights & Commentary* has summarized the four main parts of the *Catechism of the Catholic Church,* synthesized and highlighted the significant material presented in it, offered a commentary that situated the text in a contemporary setting, and suggested additional readings. Now it is time to step back and offer some final impressions and conclusions regarding this historic volume.

The vast amount of material that is contained in the *Catechism of the Catholic Church* is truly amazing. The Catechism is really a compendium, an encyclopedia of Catholic beliefs and moral teachings. Generally, it is not a book to put into the hands of students, or even a textbook from which one might teach. As Pope John Paul II has pointed out, the Catechism does not replace the many approved catechisms that have already been produced in countries throughout the world.

Modern catechesis does not begin with this text, but will be enhanced and refined by it. The Catechism will no doubt generate new catechetical materials for some time to come.

Religious educators will still be challenged to find creative and effective ways to explain the teachings of the church as they are presented in the Catechism. They will still be pressed to connect these teachings with the real-life experience of their students. They will need to find ways of using these teachings to move their students to act with integrity and with a concern for others.

Great effort will be required to adapt these teachings to various cultures throughout the world. Karl Rahner pointed out that the Second Vatican Council marked the beginning of a new "world church." But "world church" no longer means, as it did in the past, the presence of European Catholicism throughout the world. Today the gospel message is being expressed in the languages of many different nations and in forms appropriate to many different cultures. The Christian tradition is becoming inculturated. It is being shaped by the milieu in which it exists.

History shows that inculturation is not really a new phenomenon in the church. The Christian tradition was Jewish in its beginnings. Then it took on the cultural notions and ways of Rome, Greece, and the various ethnic groups of Europe. Today the gospel tradition is expressed and lived as Asian, African, and Latino. Christianity impacts and is impacted by many other ethnic and national groups throughout the world. There is much work to be done in order to adapt the teachings of the Catechism to all these peoples.

For many years to come the Catechism will stand as a benchmark for contemporary Catholic belief. It draws together ideas from many of the church's best thinkers: the early Fathers, Augustine, Aquinas, and a number of the more recent popes, especially John Paul II. The text generously quotes the scriptures, the pronouncements of the major councils of the church, and some of the writings of the saints. Significantly, the Catechism draws freely from the documents of Vatican II, which brought about some of the most profound changes in the church in many centuries. In all, one is struck by the beauty and richness of the Catholic tradition. In the Catechism's extensive presentation of the faith one can see the gospel of Jesus Christ shining through in all its simplicity and grandeur.

Although the Catechism is a treasure of resources on most major areas of the Catholic tradition, there is much more that can be said about the Christian message. There is the vast amount of fine biblical criticism that has been done on both the Hebrew Scriptures and the New Testament over the last half century. There is a large body of historical and theological writings that has significantly re-interpreted and reapplied the Christian tradition. The great theologians of the Second Vatican Council like Karl Rahner, Henri de Lubac, Yves Congar, Edward Schillebeeckx, John Courtney Murray, and Bernard Häring, as well as many other contemporary theologians offer invaluable insights to the Catholic teacher, pastor, or interested church members.

The prophetic voices of Teilhard de Chardin, Dorothy Day, Thomas Merton, Gustavo Gutiérrez, and many others provide a new and hopeful vision and call people to prayer, peace, and justice. There are also the Protestant theological giants of our times, scholars like Paul Tillich, Karl Barth, Dietrich Bonhoeffer, and others. Much is to be learned from all these important thinkers.

Years of fruitful dialogue among Catholics, Protestants, and Jews have rendered new understanding and appreciation for other religious traditions. There is much to be gained from studying the beliefs and customs of Buddhism, Hinduism, Islam, and the Native American religions. What has been learned from all these respected churches and religions should be shared with future generations of Catholics.

Numerous valuable materials are published today on pastoral theology, religious education, spirituality, morality, biblical studies, social justice, and ecology. A growing number of feminist theologians are providing Catholics with fresh perspectives in many areas of scripture and theology. Indeed the Catechism can be augmented with many such resources, as well as by the insights of contemporary art, science, psychology, literature, social science, and modern pedagogy. The context for today's catechesis is, after all, the contemporary world with all its challenges and complexities.

Liberation theology, a gospel perspective that has arisen among those who live in poverty and oppression, has much to offer the global church. As the liberation movement spreads throughout the world, it will continue to awaken many of the downtrodden to the freeing power of God in their midst. In one form or another liberation theology will continue to be a stimulus to all Catholics for acting on behalf of the disenfranchised.

One can only wonder what the future will hold for the Catholic Church as it enters the third millennium. Will there be a pope from a Third World country? Will there be a Vatican Council III, or perhaps a Jerusalem II? What does the future hold for the church in the developing countries or in Eastern Europe?

How will AIDS affect the church? What changes will come about in ministry and in the shape of local faith communities?

The *Catechism of the Catholic Church* moves with us into uncharted waters and serves as an invaluable compendium of our traditions and basic beliefs. Like the good steward mentioned in the gospel, this Catechism, as well as its successors, will continue to bring forth things both old and new. We can only hope that the Catechism and this book of highlights and commentary will contribute in some way to the enterprise of catechesis.